D0551607

DEATH WITH DIGNITY FAQs

(FREQUENTLY ASKED QUESTIONS)

Rob Neils, Ph.D.

President, Dying Well Network
Professional Clinical Psychologist

KENDALL/HUNT PUBLISHING COMPANY
4050 Westmark Drive   Dubuque, Iowa 52002

Copyright © 1997 by Rob Neils

ISBN 0-7872-3611-X

All rights reserved. No part of this publication may be reproduced, stored in a retrieval system, or transmitted, in any form or by any means, electronic, mechanical, photocopying, recording, or otherwise, without the prior written permission of the copyright owner.

Printed in the United States of America
10 9 8 7 6 5 4 3 2 1

CONTENTS

ACKNOWLEDGEMENTS

Optimum philosophia et sapientia est comtemplatio de mortis.

I thank each of you who has shared your deathing with me. You are gone from "out there" but you are alive "in here." You have taught me a lot.

I thank the members of the **Dying Well Network**. You decrease suffering and increase enlightenment. You are a blessing to me and to many.

I thank hospice professionals and volunteers in the Rocky Mountain area along both sides of the U.S. and Canadian border. As I helped you, you helped me.

I thank Jeff Winikoff. We have climbed together and boldly gone where few have gone before. You're a rock!

Sandi, my soul-mate of 29 years, I thank you for affording me the time away from you and many of my spousal responsibilities while doing my "social justice" work. You help me understand that I work the issue passionately and, yes, often obsessively, but "Evil flourishes where good people fail to do their duty!" I love you. May we have 29 more years together!

Earth and Sky, you and I live and die forever.

Earth and Sky, you and I live and die together.

And even the stars die…but they twinkle first!

INTRODUCTION

Many of the most beautiful and meaningful facets of life are the way they are because they are ephemeral. When I was a student in college, often before I went to bed I would listen to Beethoven's Ninth. There was a chord in the final movement that for me lifted the entire piece to an ecstatic plane. Every time I listened, I anticipated that one chord. It lasted approximately seven seconds, and I always wished the feelings I was experiencing would never end. However, one evening I asked myself what it would be like to experience that chord forever. It was then I realized if the chord were made eternal I would develop a hatred for it. I wouldn't be able to bear listening to that chord for a day, an hour, minute or even one more measure. The chord was beautiful and meaningful because of its brief but essential relation to the entire piece. It was beautiful and meaningful because of its finitude.

So many of us live our lives striving for the infinite, for our own immortality. We refuse to acknowledge our own passing placement in the web of life, and in doing so we fail to see our own beauty. It has become our mission to forestall death. Everyday we exercise, eat right, take our vitamins in an attempt to suspend the inevitable. However, the fact remains that in the final analysis there is always death. Even people who have accepted this fact often forget their death can be controlled. We can rightfully be concerned with how and when we die. Today we have a responsibility to reconstruct our understandings of death which have been vitiated by denial and fear. To live full, meaningful lives we must embrace our mortality. We must learn to control our dying that we can die well.

Chad Clouse

PREFACE

Man is born with death in his hand. We all will die. We may be able to postpone death but we cannot avoid it. We all die of something, somewhere, somehow. Although we cannot avoid death, we can control the death caused by a terminal illness. We can determine how, when, where, and with whom we die. That is what this book is all about: Controlling dying and thereby dying well.

Acceptance of death increases the quality of life a terminally ill person has remaining. A terminally ill person lives better knowing that he or she may exercise control over the physical pain, the psychological agony and the financial devastation of dying. As founder and president of **Dying Well Network,** I have been with terminally ill persons as they hastened their death. Just before death each of them has expressed deep gratitude and a belief that he or she got to live better and possibly longer because of the option to control the time and method of dying. Each died well. One woman who had lived an "extra month once I got the monkey off my back" said, "You ought to call **Dying Well, Living and Dying Well**."

Kahil Gibran, an Arab mystic who lived in Lebanon from 1883 to 1931, wrote in The Prophet, "You would know the secret of death. But how shall you find it unless you seek it in the heart of life? For life and death are one, even as the river and the sea are one."

There are two main rules in life. The first rule is to live your life in such a way that you generate some good stories. The second rule is to live to tell the stories! The second rule is not as important as the first! May your death be a story of courage, grace and dignity!

Rob Neils, Ph.D.
Clinical Psychologist
President, **Dying Well Network**

Section 1: DEITY

1.01) Isn't physician aid-in-dying "playing God"?

This is the same argument that was used against surgery only a hundred years ago. Is open heart surgery "playing God"? Is using artificial birth control or getting a blood transfusion "playing God"? For some religions it is.

Are you "playing God" when you pull the plug...or when you put it in?

Nancy Cruzan was a 32 year-old Missouri woman who was in a persistent vegetative state for seven years after an auto accident. Her folks fought all the way up to the Supreme Court to get her off artificial nutrition and hydration. Finally it was allowed. When the day came to take the tubes out, nineteen people stormed the facility to try to put the tubes back in. They were arrested and placed in jail. Now that's "playing God"!

1.02) Hubris: Pretending to be God.

Jacob Bronowski wrote in **The Ascent of Man**,

> There is no absolute knowledge. And those who claim it, whether they are scientists or dogmatists, open the door to tragedy. All information is imperfect. We have to treat it with humility. That is the human condition.

Later, in a Public Television series based on his book, Dr. Bronowski took us viewers to a pond at the Auschwitz concentration camp. He waded into the shallow water, scooped up some of the sediment from beneath the surface, and as the "mud" dripped between his fingers, he informed us,

> This is the concentration camp and crematorium at Auschwitz. This is where people were turned into numbers. Into this pond were flushed the ashes of some four million people. And that

was not done by gas. It was done by arrogance. It was done by dogma. It was done by ignorance. When people believe that they have absolute knowledge, with no test in reality, this is how they behave. This is what men do when they aspire to the knowledge of gods.

It is critical to examine closely those who admonish others to do or not do something by saying, in effect, "God told me to tell you...." They crave absolute knowledge and power by pretending to speak for God. They crave that which they fail to realize is addicting poison: Hubris, the arch sin of speaking as the center of the universe. Behind the brightest light always lurks the deepest shadow.

It took the Roman Catholic church two and a half centuries to admit it made a mistake in condemning Galileo for saying the universe does not revolve around the earth.

1.03) What about miracles?

A miracle is properly defined as any event that helps one to believe in God or to see underlying depth. Even the commonplace can be a miracle...and usually is.

The Rev. Harry Cole went to court to have his wife, Jackie's respirator removed after a brain hemorrhage placed her in a coma. The judge refused. Six days later Jackie woke up! She suffered some short-term memory loss but otherwise was fairly well recovered. "What happened to me was truly miraculous," she exclaimed. She did not blame Harry for wanting to pull the plug. "I know he loves me," she said, adding, "I know he was never trying to do away with me." Harry didn't feel guilty about his decision. He reported, "I thought my decision was well planned, well thought out, and responsible. It was what Jackie had asked me to do."

Twenty-three year old Jerry was near death on the Oncology unit at Fresno Community Hospital. His counselor sat silently with him as he slipped into a coma. His oncologist entered the room and, seeing Jerry near death, ordered two units of blood transfused into him. The treatment worked. Jerry regained full consciousness but he was angry! He described what had happened to him as being "soul-raped." "Even if a miracle cure is found it'd be too late for me," he added. He still wanted to die...and did...three agonizing days later.

1.04) Isn't it against the commandment, "Thou shalt not kill"?

All cultures have strong prohibitions against killing. However cultures approve of killing in time of war or in defense against a life-threatening attack. The Fifth Commandment (Sixth for Roman Catholics) states simply "Thou shalt not kill." However, there are 62 verses in the Bible calling for killing as a punishment for approximately 30 various transgressions.

Aid-in-dying is not killing. Killing connotes doing something to someone against their will to end their living. Physician aid-in-dying is doing something with someone who requests it to end their dying. Murder and killing are done against the victim's will. Physician aid-in-dying is done with the wishes of the person who petitions it. Therefore the words "murder" and "killing" are inappropriate when referring to physician assistance in dying.

1.05) Is it true "Only God can give a life or take a life"?

Most fertile couples use birth control to plan pregnancies. They choose when to conceive life. The Roman Catholic church proclaims that it is wrong to practice birth control other than by the abstinence or by the "rhythm" method. Many persons do practice "artificial" birth control and would vehemently object to anyone telling them that they are wrong or "sinful" in doing so. Those who believe that birth (or death) control is wrong, need not practice it. Those persons who believe that it is wrong to ask for or give assistance-in-dying need not, and will not, request it for themselves.

However, their beliefs should not prohibit those of differing beliefs from requesting aid-in-dying.

Judge Reinhardt, writing the conclusion of the Ninth Circuit Court of Appeals in the case of Compassion In Dying versus the State of Washington, advised tolerance between those of differing beliefs.

> Those who believe strongly that death must come without physician assistance are free to follow that creed, be they doctors or patients. They are not free, however, to force their views, their religious convictions, or their philosophies on all the other members of a democratic society, and to compel those whose values differ with theirs to die painful, protracted, and agonizing deaths.

1.06) Will people change their minds on this issue?

There is a principle which is proof against all information, which is proof against all arguments, which cannot fail to keep man in everlasting ignorance. That principle is contempt, prior to investigation.

Herbert Spencer

It's not likely that someone will change his or her mind about physician aid-in-dying just by reading this or other information. Basic beliefs are resistant to change. If persons against the right-to-die were to experience a desperately needed, chosen and gentle deathing then they would have a personal experience to help alter their beliefs. The trouble is that people who are very much against deathing would not be invited to, or probably even told about, the deathing either before or after it happens.

Dying Well Network uses the present active participle "deathing" as a noun to communicate the action of hastening or facilitating death. It's a lot like "birthing." We have found the word to be neutral yet fully descriptive and adequate.

Like a dad at a birthing of his child, if he's against being in the delivery room, he will miss a life-experience, and likely won't change his beliefs about birthing.

There is another way to learn how precious a deathing is. Experience it yourself! Each terminally or incurably ill person with whom **Dying Well Network** has been during a deathing, has compared the deathing to birthing. Each has appreciated those who have risked the penalties of antiquated laws which are now being over-turned.

Would a person vehemently against the right-to-die ask for it? Not very likely, unless that person became terminally ill with no hope of recovery, no quality of life, no dignity left and no relief from pain.

A bigot is a person of prejudice or overly strong convictions, especially in matters of philosophy, politics, race or religion. Bigots are intolerant of those who have differing opinions, no matter how reasonable or popular those opinions are. Bigots fail to appreciate the valid opinions and beliefs of others.

The idea of controlling dying may offend persons with overly rigid beliefs against it but it is a reasonable and popular idea which now needs exploration. Thank you, reader, for exploring this issue.

1.07) Are all religions against aid-in-dying?

At the 1988 General Assembly of the Unitarian Universalist General Convention, that church became the only religious denomination in the world to officially resolve to

> advocate the right to self-determination in dying, and the release from civil and criminal penalties of those who, under proper safeguards, act to honor the right of the terminally ill patients to select the time of their own deaths.

Washington, California and Oregon's Death With Dignity Initiatives were officially endorsed by the Unitarian-Universalist Department of Social Responsibility. The Unitarian Universalist Association has

presented "friend of the court (amicus curiae)" briefs at the Circuit
Court of Appeals level supporting the right-to-die.

On January 29, 1996, the two hundred delegates to the annual
convention of the Episcopal Diocese of Newark adopted a
resolution calling suicide a "moral choice" for those who are
terminally ill or those living in persistent or progressive pain. The
next national Episcopal Church convention will debate the issue.
The Episcopal Church has about 2,500,000 members.

Ninth Circuit Court of Appeals Judge Reinhardt documented the
early Christians' very different attitude about hastening death.

> The early Christians saw death as an escape from the
> tribulations of a fallen existence and as the doorway to heaven.
> The Christian impulse to martyrdom reached its height with the
> Donatists, who were so eager to enter into martyrdom that they
> were eventually declared heretics. Gibbon, in the Decline and
> Fall of the Roman Empire, described them this way, "They
> sometimes forced their way into courts of justice and compelled
> the affrighted judge to give orders for their execution. They
> frequently stopped travelers on the public highways and obliged
> them to inflict the stroke of martyrdom by promise of a reward,
> if they consented—and by the threat of instant death, if they
> refused to grant so singular a favor."

The early Christians faced death by lions and gladiators, not only
without fear, but with the fervent hope that they would soon be
released from earth to heaven. Perhaps in present time Christians
against hastening death will see terminally ill friends and loved ones
welcome death and thereby convert to be like the early Christian
martyrs who taught the Romans that death was not only nothing to
fear but actually something to welcome.

Judge Reinhardt also recognized that some religious persons will
have "great distress" about physician aid-in-dying.

We also acknowledge that judicial acceptance of physician-assisted suicide would cause many sincere persons with strong moral or religious convictions great distress.

1.08) How about Hope?

When the Greek gods created the earth they kept, captured in a box, all the grievous ills and ailments that could afflict us humans. You remember the story...about Pandora, to whom the gods gave the box for safe keeping. And you remember how curious Pandora opened the box thereby releasing all the ills and evils upon the world.

Poor Pandora collapsed into a guilt-anguished puddle on the floor next to the box from which she had just released all those horribles. As she slumped, she closed the lid, but too late.

I bet you don't remember "the rest of the story." Here it is.

As Pandora lay there, she heard from within the box a soft buzzing sound coming from the now closed box. She was, remarkably, still curious, even in her dreadful anguish. But she had learned. Yet the buzzing continued.

Should she open the box? Would you?

She did.

And as her eyes rose above the walls of the box she saw, buzzing in the corner, Hope, the last gift of the gods.

Without Hope we are in shambles.

But when we're well, and okay, and feeling good we don't notice Hope. We take Hope for granted.

And when we're well and feeling good but with someone who isn't so well or feeling so good we forget that their Hope is different from ours. Listen to the changing Hope of an ailing person: "I hope nothing's really wrong; I hope the doctor can tell me what's wrong; I hope the doctor can fix me or can aid me in my responsibility to regain the most health I can; I hope the next 'cure' works; I hope I won't be in too much pain; I hope I won't be a burden to others; I hope I can keep being myself; I hope I can die peacefully; I hope to die."

"You should never take away hope," goes the maxim. That's right. But Hope doesn't desert a patient no matter what we say. She just changes in a never-ending, often slowing, intimate dance of life...and, finally, death.

Hope accompanies us from the cradle to the grave. She helps us accept life and death. She teaches us that life is good and death can be good.

When in counsel with an ailing fellow human, match your hope with the patient's. Let the patient know that Spring follows Winter. And don't deny Winter. Winter isn't without Hope. Winter dies that Spring may live. Every beginning requires an ending.

Be careful to match your hope for the patient with the patient's hope for self. And when a patient is ready to die be careful not to foist false hope, a hope projected from a well person onto a very sick one. It's hard to allow hope to change from cure to termination. Freud said we can't really imagine our own death because it's so foreign. It's also hard to imagine the death of another...and to imagine that they could actually desire it. Ernest Becker wrote a most challenging and rewarding, Pulitzer prize winning book, The Denial of Death, on this subject. It is "must" reading.

Refer terminally ill persons to Hospice.

Hospice's middle name is Hope (HOsPicE). They're ready to serve the sick (hoSpICe). Hospice is "Hope for the sick." Hospice matches sick people with their Hope, especially if their Hope is to die at home. Hospice will not help people die, but they will keep people as comfortable as possible while they die. Hospices' charter philosophy states plainly and simply that hospices "will neither prolong nor hasten death."

1.09) Does the right to die ignore the sanctity of life?

Life is precious; so is the quality of life.

Those who want to hang onto life to the bitter end have the privilege to do so. We respect their choices and we expect them to respect ours.

1.10) Doesn't pain build character?

Some persons argue that a terminally ill patient builds character by suffering. The Pro-Life Catechism of the Roman Catholic church boldly makes such an assertion.

Let's not just automatically discount this statement; let's look at it with an open mind to see what we can learn.

For many centuries, while dying was usually very painful and medicine did not have adequate means to relieve pain, persons often died in physical pain and psychological agony. Their priest could comfort them by telling them that their pain had meaning because it helped them to appreciate the pain that Jesus had to go through on the cross. These were loving words of comfort, the best treatment available. What was once loving practice has now become outmoded dogma. It is no longer necessary to die in pain. The past consolation need not become a present command.

Character is another term for style, a person's consistent behavior patterns and habits. If a person took care to have a good life, consistent style would indicate that person would take care to have a good death: "Good life; good death." "Good death" is what "euthanasia" means, literally.

1.11) Is hastening death unethical?

In the March 30, 1989 issue of the <u>New England Journal of Medicine</u>, a prestigious journal, ten of twelve physicians impaneled from medical schools in Harvard, Texas, Chicago, Minneapolis, Virginia, San Francisco, Pittsburgh, and the Mayo Clinic, agreed that "it is not immoral for a physician to assist in the rational suicide of the terminally ill person." The ten concluded, "It is ethical to prescribe pills knowing the intent of the patient to use the pills to end his life." The panel of doctors noted that some physicians

> do assist patients who request it, either by prescribing sleeping pills with knowledge of their intended use or by discussing the required doses and methods of administration with the patient. The frequency with which such actions are undertaken is unknown but they are certainly not rare (even though assisting a suicide is a felony crime in about 30 of the 52 states in the United States).

Margaret Pabst Battin, author of <u>Ethical Issues in Suicide</u>, considers the right of a terminally or incurably ill person to hasten death as a natural, fundamental right because it promotes human dignity. Such rights as liberty, freedom of speech, education, and freedom of religion are not "proven" by argument. They are described as inherent, "proving themselves" and "self-evident." Natural rights are grasped as much by intuition as by proofs. Pabst Battin offers the following salient quote from Rousseau's Saint-Preux,

> The more I reflect, the more I am convinced that the question may be reduced to this fundamental proposition: Every man has a right by nature to pursue what he thinks good, and avoid what he thinks evil, in all respects which are not injurious to others. When our life, therefore, becomes a misery to ourselves and is of advantage to no one, we are at liberty to put an end to our being. If there is any such thing as a clear and self-evident principle, certainly this is one.

1.12) Is hastening death anti-religious?

Hastening the death of a terminally ill person is not anti-religious; it is as deeply and personally religious as can be. It takes place between a dying person and his or her God, ethical standards and philosophical approach. It is an action guided, but not governed, by what one has learned. It is not bound only by doctrine. Therefore some religious organizations may fear the loss of control over an action which is controlled by individual conscience rather than institutional standards.

The choice to facilitate deathing is intensely and deeply personal. It is an elemental choice and act grounded in the depth of who the person has been, who the person is now and who the person will or will not become. It is a solitary choice. Yet it takes into consideration the needs of others, but it is not dictated by the beliefs of others. It is therefore not easily controlled by organized religion which may therefore see it as a threat to its power and control rather than see it as an opportunity for spiritual connection. If facilitating death is rejected by an organized religion then that religion blocks itself from being with the dying person at the point of greatest need. In fact, to deny a person the comfort of a loving and supporting community at the time of a deathing can be seen as anti-religious.

Birthing is sanctioned, "sanctified," by the religious ceremony of naming or christening. Mating is sanctioned, "sanctified," by the religious ceremony of marriage. Can not deathing also be sanctioned, "sanctified," by a religious ceremony? Can not a church offer sanction, "sanctuary," for a person requesting to die...not alone, but within a loving circle of friends, within a religious community?

Facilitating death is a religious choice. The choice is irreconcilable, final, and most gravely important, not only to the person making it, but also to the surviving community left behind. It is, as are all religious acts, a matter of individual conscience grounded within the social structure which guides but does not control it. At greatest depth, all religious acts are a matter of individual responsibility balanced, and, at best, supported by the religious and cultural environment in which it takes place. Facilitating death is, therefore, a most profoundly religious act.

It is also a religious act for each person attending a deathing. Can you imagine attending a deathing? Ultimate questions must be addressed: "Is this right?" "What can and will I do while present at a deathing?" "Is this in harmony with my beliefs and way of life?" "How do I feel about this and how will I feel about it later as I grieve the passing of this loved one?" and "Does this affect my own life's journey in a negative or positive way?"

Wouldn't a deathing best take place within a religious setting? How could it not? The setting in which a deathing takes place becomes a religious setting whether or not it takes place in a church because a deathing is a religious act. (Please see section 6.05 "The cases of Rev. John Evans and Betty Drumheller" later in this book.)

Religions which control membership through guilt and intimidation are unlikely to study or endorse the Death With Dignity movement. They fear allowing the free, individual conscience to be the primary religious conduit, especially if it is uncontrolled by the church. However, many faiths, especially the Methodist, Presbyterian, Episcopalian, United Church of Christ, Unitarian-Universalist, and Jewish, are studying the Death With Dignity concept. Numerous Christian and Jewish organizations have endorsed the Death With Dignity Initiatives in Washington, California and Oregon.

Often ministers, rabbis and other religious leaders guide loved ones at the bedside of a dying person, asking that God's will be done, that death come. Aren't we, too, responsible for seeing that God's will be done? Prayer which leaves everything to God, without taking up the personal responsibility to make the prayer come true, is shy of the dynamic mutuality between God and the person praying. Asking God alone to be responsible, when the person praying won't be responsible, lacks credibility. A saint once advised, "Pray like everything depends on God, then work like everything depends on you." Prayer carries within itself an obligation to act.

Section 2: DOCTOR

2.01) Why should it be doctors who help people hasten death?

They are the only ones trained and legally able to prescribe medications. They have experience in end-of-life treatment. They have a strong interest in preserving life when there is a probability that some quality of life remains. They are regulated by law and professional ethics. They have a system of peer review. Many of them are already doing it, but in secret, without regulation.

2.02) Would physicians give aid-in-dying if it were legal?

Dr. Shapiro reported a survey of Wisconsin physicians which found that 27% of them said they would be willing to perform euthanasia if it were legalized. Catholic and fundamentalist physicians were less likely to be willing. Family and general practice physicians were most willing because, the researchers believed, they tend to have long-term relationships with their patients.

In 1995, the Center for Ethics in Health Care at the Oregon Health Sciences University in Portland surveyed 2,761 of the state's physicians after Oregon voters passed Measure 16 allowing physician aid-in-dying. Dr. Lee reported the following numbers:

• 73% believed that terminally ill persons have the right to suicide;

• 66% believed that physician assisted suicide is ethical;

• 60% believed that physician assisted suicide should be legal;

• 46% would be willing to comply with a patient's valid request;

• 21% had been asked for a lethal prescription in the past year;

• 7% had written a lethal prescription before Measure 16 passed.

Dr. Bachman reported that of 1,119 Michigan physicians surveyed in 1994 and 1995 40% favored a law permitting physician-assisted suicide. When asked if they themselves would be willing to participate in physician assisted suicide or in voluntary euthanasia, 52% said they would not, 13% said they might participate only in assisted suicide and 22% said they might participate in both.

The July 14, 1994, New England Journal of Medicine contained a "Special Article" entitled, "Attitudes Toward Assisted Suicide and Euthanasia Among Physicians in Washington State." The results:

> Of the 1,355 eligible physicians who received our questionnaire, 938 (69%) responded. Forty-eight percent of the respondents agreed with the statement that euthanasia is never ethically justified, and 42 percent disagreed. Fifty-four percent thought euthanasia should be legal in some situations, but only 33% stated they would be willing to perform euthanasia. Thirty-nine percent of the respondents agreed with the statement that physician-assisted suicide is never ethically justified, and 50 percent disagreed. Fifty-three percent thought assisted suicide should be legal in some situations, but only 40 percent stated that they would be willing to assist a patient in committing suicide.

A January 1988 poll of 7,000 physicians in Colorado polled by the Center for Health Ethics and Policy at the University of Colorado found,

> •14% have helped patients stockpile lethal doses of drugs;

> •60% had had patients for whom euthanasia would have been justified if legal;

> •35% would have injected a lethal drug dose had such a practice been legal.

A sample of 600 physicians in California in 1988 found that 95% of them who have been asked to hasten death agreed that such a request can be "rational." Nearly 23% said they had already helped people die, some of them have aided three or more patients to die. Forty percent said they thought other doctors hastened the death of some patients despite the legal prohibition.

The American Journal of Respiratory and Critical Care Medicine reported in February, 1996, that a survey of 879 doctors in adult intensive care units throughout the United States found that 96% of the doctors had discontinued medical treatment by either withdrawing or withholding treatment with the expectation that the patient would die as a result. Of the total, 85% had done so at least once in the last year.

Dying Well Network knows physicians in the Spokane, Washington area who are willing to aid terminally ill persons to hasten death, but does not connect terminally ill persons with these courageous physicians. Persons seeking aid-in-dying are directed to their own physicians.

Ninth Circuit Court of Appeals Judge Reinhardt noted the following:

> The Oregon AMA refrained from taking a position on a successful ballot initiative to legalize physician assisted suicide because its membership was sharply divided on whether to back or oppose the measure. Many more doctors support physician-assisted suicide but without openly advocating a change in the legal treatment of the practice. A recent study of Oregon physicians found that 60% of those who responded believed that physician-assisted suicide should be legal.

A recent study of attitudes among physicians in Michigan, where the state legislature adopted a law banning assisted-suicide as a result of Dr. Jack Kevorkian's activities, found that only 17.2% of the physicians who responded favored a law prohibiting assisted-suicide. Almost all the rest supported one of three options: legalizing physician-assisted suicide (38.9%); permitting the medical profession to regulate the practice (16.1%); or leaving decisions about physician-assisted suicide to the doctor-patient relationship

(16.6%). Thus over 70% of the Michigan doctors answering the poll appear to believe that professional ethics do not preclude doctors from engaging in acts that today are classified as "assisted suicide." Even among those doctors who oppose assisted suicide, medical ethics do not lie at the heart of their objections. The "most important personal characteristic" separating those doctors from their colleagues was a "strong religious identification."

In the March 27, 1996 Journal of the American Medical Association, in an article entitled "Physician-Assisted Suicide and Euthanasia in Washington State," authors Back et al. report that of the 828 Washington physicians queried, 12% of the responding physicians had had one or more explicit requests from patients for physician aid-in-dying or euthanasia. Physician aid-in-dying was defined as "the physician prescribe(ing) medications that the patient could use with the primary intention of ending his or her life." Of the 156 patients requesting physician aid-in-dying, 38 (24%) were given prescriptions for a fatal dose of medication. Twenty-one used the prescription to hasten death. Euthanasia was defined as "the physician inject(ing) medication with the primary intention of ending the patient's life." Fifty-eight patients requested euthanasia. Fourteen (24%) received active euthanasia and died as a result.

Oncologists and physicians in internal medicine received requests more frequently than did primary care physicians. Most of the requesting patients were men over age 65 who had known their physician for more than 12 months and were expected to live for no more than 6 months. Cancer, neurological diseases (like Multiple Sclerosis), and AIDS accounted for 69% of the diagnoses. Heart disease was not a diagnosis associated with requests for assistance in dying, even though heart disease accounts for more deaths (29%) than cancer (25%) and AIDS (1.2%).

Patients gave the following reasons for wanting to die:

- future loss of control, 159 patients (77% of the total);
- being a burden, 156 (75%);

- being dependent on others for some or all personal care, 154 (74%);

- loss of dignity, 149 (72%);

- being restricted to bed more than 50% of the time, 119 (57%);

- experiencing severe depression or depressed mood, 114 (55%);

- experiencing severe suffering, 108 (52%);

- experiencing severe physical discomfort other than pain, 103 (50%);

- experiencing severe pain, 73 (35%);

- worried about medical costs, 48 (23%).

Note that pain is the least often given reason for wanting to hasten death. Loss of control and dignity, being a burden and dependent, and being restricted to bed most of the time are the reasons most often given for wanting to hasten death.

However, physicians were least likely to aid those who mentioned non-physical reasons and most likely to aid when physical pain was one of the primary reasons for asking. Physicians declined to give aid-in-dying to 114 of the 156 patients (73%) asking for it. They refused for the following reasons:

- the symptoms were potentially treatable, 26 (23%);

- the patient was depressed, 22 (19%);

- the patient was expected to live longer than six months, 21 (18%);

- the degree of suffering "didn't justify" the request, 13 (11%);

- the physician didn't know the patient "well enough," 6 (5%);

- the physician "felt that physicians should never participate in physician-suicide," 34 (30%);

- the physician was worried about legal consequences, 17 (15%).

Physicians who refused their patients "described relationships of increasing detachment" and reported that the patients had left them for another primary care physician by the time they died. Only 15% of the physicians sought second opinions. Only 24% referred patients to psychiatric or psychological evaluation and treatment. Two patients received aid-in-dying after only one request. Only one physician sought the advice of an ethics committee but "found the discussion to be so constrained by legal considerations that it was not helpful."

The findings from this Washington study raise serious questions concerning the quality of decision-making and treatment in end-of-life-decisions. Regulation and quality control are needed but are unlikely to occur until physician aid-in-dying is defined by law and administrative guidance. Legalizing physician aid-in-dying will increase public safety by bringing it out of the closet into the "rude eye of public scrutiny."

Judge Reinhardt, of the Ninth Circuit Court of Appeals, noted that many physicians already give assistance in dying,

> Running beneath the official history of legal condemnation of physician-assisted suicide is a strong undercurrent of a time-honored but hidden practice of physicians helping terminally ill patients to hasten their deaths. According to a survey by the American Society of Internal Medicine, one doctor in five said he had assisted in a patient's suicide. Accounts of doctors who have helped their patients end their lives have appeared both in professional journals and in the daily press.

Gratitude is expressed by this author to those physicians who are presently willing to put their patient's needs in front of their own. We need to legalize physician aid-in-dying not only for patients' needs but for doctors' too!

On Tuesday, December 10, 1996, Andrew Nowalk, president of the 30,000-member American Medical Student Association, filed a legal brief before the U.S. Supreme Court supporting physician-assisted suicide. Medical students are the physicians of the future!

2.03) Won't nurses or other health providers end up giving aid-in-dying?

No, once aid-in-dying is regulated only physicians will be allowed to give physician aid-in-dying.

Physicians cannot practice outside the area of their training and experience. An "eye doctor" can't do open-heart surgery because the "eye doctor" isn't credentialed and privileged to do so. If the "eye doctor" practiced outside his or her area of competency then that doctor would be liable for professional and legal sanctions. Before a doctor can practice medicine, he or she has to meet state regulations. Before a doctor can work in a hospital or other health care institution, he or she must be credentialed and privileged. To be credentialed, the doctor must supply the necessary proof that he or she has accomplished the necessary training and experience to do the job for which he or she is making application. To be privileged, the doctor must demonstrate the skills necessary to perform in the position for which he or she applies.

Although aid-in-dying is just now being established by voter initiative and through the courts, it is already being done, but in secret, almost always without supervision or public scrutiny. Individual rights must always be balanced with the safety of others. That is why physician aid-in-dying needs so badly to be legalized and regulated.

As it is now, some nurses do hasten the death of their patients, without supervision and, at times, even without the request of the patient! In the May 23, 1996, New England Journal of Medicine, Dr. David Asch reported the results of the survey he sent to 1,600 critical care nurses in the United States. Of the 1139 nurses who responded (71 percent), 852 said they practiced exclusively in intensive care units for adults in the United States. Of these 852 nurses, 141 (17 percent) reported that they had received requests from patients or family members to perform euthanasia or assist in suicide; 129 (16 percent of those for whom data were available) reported that they had engaged in such practices; and an additional 35 (4 percent) reported that they had hastened a patient's death by only pretending to provide life-sustaining treatment ordered by a physician. Some nurses reported engaging in these practices without the request or advance knowledge of physicians or others. The method of euthanasia most commonly described was the administration of a high dose of an opiate to a terminally ill patient.

It is important that administrative law be created to regulate physician aid-in-dying.

Nurses view patients dying differently than doctors do. Liaschenko and Davis report in the Journal of Medical Philosophy that nurses focus on the patients' suffering while doctors focus on a "cultural tradition of morality in which a universal standard always assumes precedence over the particularities of a situation." Nurses view death as "the end of life." Physicians view death as "the enemy in any circumstance." Nurses accent "care" while doctors accent "cure." Doctors tend to be "technology bound" while nurses are person-centered. Doctors maintain "scientific objectivity" while nurses are much more likely to practice "hands on" care. Doctors tend to view suffering as a "problem to be solved, molded and manipulated." Nurses view suffering as a "lived and shared experience." In summary, the main distinguishing difference between physicians and nurses is the difference between "the absolutist and the contextualist ethical perspectives."

2.04) Would people think of physicians as killers?

Some opponents argue that, "If physicians become killers, they will lose the respect of their patients and many people will be afraid to go to a doctor." To the contrary, a doctor who helps mercifully to end suffering, gains respect because of the compassion such an act conveys. Families are grateful to physicians who help them in such a grave situation. It affirms their respect for the doctor and for the medical profession; it does not diminish it.

People appreciate a veterinarian who "puts to sleep" a pet to end suffering. These people do not suspect that this same veterinarian will kill other pets brought in to them for healing. People loyally return to their veterinarian "who is there when you need it the most."

It is tragic that as laws in most states stand now, there are caring physicians who have to jeopardize their license and freedom to give terminally ill patients assistance in dying. The physicians who currently give assistance in dying are courageous. They place their patient's welfare above their own! They help us, so let us help them by making physician aid-in-dying legal. Then they will not have to risk their license and their freedom as they do now.

Ninth Circuit Court of Appeals Judge Reinhardt dispelled the argument that patients wouldn't trust physicians who would give aid-in-dying.

> The state has a legitimate interest in assuring the integrity of the medical profession, an interest that includes prohibiting physicians from engaging in conduct that is at odds with their role as healers. We do not believe that the integrity of the medical profession would be threatened in any way by the vindication of the liberty interest at issue here. Rather, it is the existence of a statute that criminalizes the provision of medical assistance to patients in need that could create conflicts with the doctors' professional obligations and make covert criminals out of honorable, dedicated, and compassionate individuals.

> The assertion that the legalization of physician-assisted suicide will erode the commitment of doctors to help their patients rests both on an ignorance of what numbers of doctors have been doing for a considerable time and on a misunderstanding of the proper function of a physician. As we have previously noted, doctors have been discreetly helping terminally ill patients

hasten their deaths for decades and probably centuries, while acknowledging privately that there was no other medical purpose to their actions. They have done so with the tacit approval of a substantial percentage of both the public and the medical profession, and without in any way diluting their commitment to their patients.

More important, regardless of the AMA or its position, experience shows that most doctors can readily adapt to a changing legal climate. Once the Court held that a woman has a constitutional right to have an abortion, doctors began performing abortions routinely and the ethical integrity of the medical profession remained undiminished. Similarly, following the recognition of a constitutional right to assisted suicide, we believe that doctors would engage in the permitted practice when appropriate, and that the integrity of the medical profession would survive without blemish. Patients who are concerned about the possibility that they will suffer an unwanted agonizing death because of a doctor's unwillingness to provide them with the medication they need would have the opportunity to select a doctor whose view of the physician's role comports with theirs.

Given the similarity between what doctors are now permitted to do and what the plaintiffs assert they should be permitted to do, we see no risk at all to the integrity of the profession. This is a conclusion that is shared by a growing number of doctors who openly support physician-assisted suicide and proclaim it to be fully compatible with the physicians' calling and with their commitment and obligation to help the sick.

On April 2, 1996 Judge Roger J. Miner, writing a unanimous decision for the Second Circuit Court of Appeals striking down New York's law banning doctors from giving aid-in-dying, simply stated,

Physicians do not fulfill the role of 'killer' by prescribing drugs to hasten death any more than they do by disconnecting life-support systems.

2.05) Is it a violation of the Hippocratic Oath?

Another argument against the Death With Dignity movement is that physicians would violate the Hippocratic Oath if they performed physician assistance in dying.

Not all physicians graduating from American medical schools take the Hippocratic oath: Only 60% do; 40% do not. The Hippocratic Oath has guided physicians since the fifth century BCE, back when medicine was terribly entwined with superstition and decadent religiosity. The oath actually begins by calling many of the Greek Gods by name to witness the oath. The oath later states, "I will neither give a deadly drug to anybody, if asked for, nor will I make a suggestion to this effect." One must remember that, at that time in ancient Greece, it was fashionable to commit suicide if one had embarrassed himself or his family in the eyes of the society. Hippocrates' prohibition was against assisting in a suicide, not against giving assistance in dying.

Hippocrates wrote in his treatise, Epidemics, "When a doctor can do no good, he must be kept from doing harm." A physician who insists on "keeping persons alive" against their wishes actually undermines peoples' respect for the profession. If Hippocrates were taken into a modern-day Intensive Care Unit where people are hooked up to machines that prolong their dying he likely would be appalled. He likely would remind doctors of their credo: "First do no harm."

The Hypocratic Oath also expressly prohibits physicians from "using the knife" (performing any surgery) or teaching women the medical arts. So, if doctors are really that serious about following the Hippocratic Oath, they should prohibit females from medical practice and not perform surgery!

Judge Reinhardt of the Ninth Circuit Court of Appeals noted the
following:

> Twenty years ago, the AMA contended that performing
> abortions violated the Hippocratic Oath; today, it claims that
> assisting terminally ill patients to hasten their death does
> likewise. Clearly, the Hippocratic Oath can have no greater
> import in deciding the constitutionality of physician assisted-
> suicide than it did in determining whether women had a
> constitutional right to have an abortion.

Medical science has developed the technology to prolong living to
such a point that it really is no longer prolonging living, but
prolonging dying. Medical technology must be used wisely.
Medical knowledge at times outdistances its wisdom. Knowledge
guides the proper use of experience. Wisdom guides the proper use
of knowledge. It is unwise to use medical knowledge to prolong
dying.

Terminally ill persons are often trapped in a painful dying process
with little dignity left them. As Woody Allen said, "I don't fear
death; I just don't want to be around when it happens!"

No physician or facility would have to comply with assisting a
terminally ill person hasten dying. They could transfer the patient
to another treatment source. If they objected to having to transfer
care to another, obliging physician, they would need to explain their
ethical concerns to the patient who would retain the right to
discontinue and transfer care. The responsibility of medical
treatment rests mutually with the patient and physician, not with
just the physician. If a Roman Catholic physician refused to
prescribe birth control pills to his patient and refused to transfer her
to someone who would, then there would still be a responsibility
owed the patient to explain the ethical dilemma and then to accept
the patient's decision to stay or leave. Then it becomes the
patient's responsibility to either resolve the issue with the physician
or seek alternative care even if not transferred. The refusing

physician would not, however, have the right to withhold information from the next treating physician as long as the information was properly requested.

2.06) Does adequate care make it unnecessary?

First, to control untreatable pain is not the only or even the main reason why terminally ill adults request physician aid-in-dying. Lack of dignity and the desire to have control over the dying process are more likely to be the reasons behind a request to hasten death.

However, let's look at the pain issue.

The April 1990 Journal of Pain and Symptom Management reported that, especially during the last four weeks of life, 60 to 90% of patients report moderate to severe pain at "an intensity sufficient to impair physical function, mood, and sociability substantially." Of the 90 terminally ill patients in this study, twenty-two openly discussed the possibility of suicide and four outrightly requested euthanasia. All who discussed suicide had a "progressive disease with accumulating disability...(and) had neither the hope of prolonged survival nor of return of normal functioning." Two of the 90 patients actually ended their own lives. The researchers expressed their concern,

> Our experience suggests that it is extremely important to set realistic goals for pain relief lest unrealistic goals increase the level of frustration experienced by the patient, family and staff. For most patients, freedom from pain with activity is unrealistic.

Even St. Christopher's Hospice in England, considered one of the most advanced hospices in the world, can't always control pain. They report that about 2.5% of their patients die in poor pain control. The physician who brags that he or she can "definitely control the pain of dying 100% of the time" is right because a dying patient can be medicated into deep unconsciousness where pain is no longer felt. Such "control" is appropriate only for those who would want such treatment. But, for those who ask, "What's the purpose of keeping the body going when the person's gone?" such treatment would be reprehensible and rejected. Not everyone places more value on the life within a person than on the person him or herself. Why keep the life alive when the person's dead?

On the other hand, needless suffering is imposed on the terminally ill by physicians too afraid to administer adequate pain medication. Their fear that the patient will become addicted is groundless and prevents good care. There is an extreme difference between dependence and addiction. Almost all people who become dependent on pain medications can wean off them without developing an addiction. People dependent on pain medications take the medication to ease their pain. People who are addicted take the medication for its mood and mind-altering effects. Dependence does not cause addiction. Commonly expressed, "You don't see terminally ill people out robbing banks to get money for more pain meds."

2.07) Would doctors quit fighting death and would research funds dry up?

Judge Reinhardt of the Ninth Circuit Court of Appeals addressed this highly improbable concern.

> We are...aware of the concern that doctors become hardened to the inevitability of death and to the plight of terminally ill patients, and that they will treat requests to die in a routine and impersonal manner, rather than affording the careful, thorough, individualized attention that each request deserves. The day of the family doctor who made house calls and knew the frailties and strengths of each family member is long gone. So, too, in the main, is the intense personal interest that doctors used to take in their patients' welfare and activities. Doctors like the rest of society face constantly increasing pressures, and may not always have the patience to deal with the elderly, some of whom can be both difficult and troublesome. Nevertheless,

there are many doctors who specialize in geriatric care and there are many more who are not specialists but who treat elderly patients with great compassion and sensitivity. We believe that most, if not all, doctors would not assist a terminally ill patient to hasten his death as long as there were any reasonable chance of alleviating the patient's suffering or enabling him to live under tolerable conditions. We also believe that physicians would not assist a patient to end his life if there were any significant doubt about the patient's true wishes. To do so would be contrary to the physicians' fundamental training, their conservative nature, and the ethics of their profession. In any case, since doctors are highly-regulated professionals, it should not be difficult for the state or the profession itself to establish rules and procedures that will ensure that the occasional negligent or careless recommendation by a licensed physician will not result in an uninformed or erroneous decision by the patient or his family.

Judge Reinhardt also dispelled the concern that research funding would dry up as physician aid-in-dying becomes legal and used.

Some argue that the relentless search for new and better treatments for the terminally ill might be undermined by permitting physicians to help terminally ill patients hasten their deaths. We put no stock in this argument. As is shown by the experience of countless patients suffering from cancer and AIDS, most patients are not willing to give up hope until they have exhausted all possibilities provided by established treatments and in addition have tried any available experimental ones. We are certain that there will be neither a shortage of patients willing to volunteer for controlled studies of new medications and treatments nor of researchers equally willing to develop new forms and manners of treatment.

2.08) Would callous doctors kill troublesome patients?

No. Doctors have laws and ethical guidelines they must follow. They are accountable to professional, institutional, and governmental review.

In addition, Death With Dignity legislation, like Oregon's Measure 16, require that there be witnesses to the patient's request. Not only must the witnesses affirm that the patient is qualified, but they, themselves must meet specific requirements. Here's what Oregon's voters passed.

1. A valid request for medication under this Act shall be insubstantially the form described in Section 6 of this Act, signed and dated by the patient and witnessed by at least two individuals who, in the presence of the patient, attest that to the best of their knowledge and belief the patient is capable, acting voluntarily, and is not being coerced to sign the request.

2. One of the witnesses shall be a person who is not: a relative of the patient by blood, marriage or adoption; a person who at the time the request is signed would be entitled to any portion of the estate of the qualified patient upon death under any will or by operation of law; or an owner, operator or employee of a health care facility where the qualified patient is receiving medical treatment or is a resident.

3. The patient's attending physician at the time the request is signed shall not be a witness.

4. If the patient is a patient in a long term care facility at the time the written request is made, one of the witnesses shall be an individual designated by the facility and having the qualifications specified by the Department of Human Resources by rule.

Physicians who give aid-in-dying would have to keep records on the procedure. These records would be subject to review as appropriate. Oregon physicians would have to keep the following medical records and documentation as required by Measure 16.

The following shall be documented or filed in the patient's medical record:

1. All oral requests by a patient for medication to end his or her life in a humane and dignified manner;

2. All written requests by a patient for medication to end his or her life in a humane and dignified manner;

3. The attending physician's diagnosis and prognosis, determination that the patient is capable, acting voluntarily and has made an informed decision;

4. The consulting physician's diagnosis and prognosis, and verification that the patient is capable, acting voluntarily and has made an informed decision;

5. A report of the outcome and determinations made during counseling, if performed;

6. The attending physician's offer to the patient to rescind his or her request at the time of the patient's second oral request pursuant to Section 3.06; and,

7. A note by the attending physician indicating that all requirements under this Act have been met and indicating the steps taken to carry out the request, including a notation of the medication prescribed.

2.09) Aren't doctors supposed to kill the pain, but not the patient?

This argument is also expressed as the "unintended consequences" and "double effect" arguments.

Judge Reinhardt of the Ninth Circuit Court of Appeals addressed the question of "double effect" as follows:

Physicians routinely and openly provide medication to
terminally ill patients with the knowledge that it will have a
"double effect"—reduce the patient's pain and hasten his death.
"Decisions Near the End of Life," a report by the Council on
Ethical and Judicial Affairs of the American Medical
Association, provides an informative discussion of "double
effect." The euphemistic use of "possible" and "may" may salve
the conscience of the AMA, but it does not change the realities
of the practice of medicine or the legal consequences that would
normally flow from the commission of an act one has reason to
believe will likely result in the death of another. In the case of
"double effect" we excuse the act or, to put it more accurately,
we find the act acceptable, not because the doctors sugarcoat
the facts in order to permit society to say that they couldn't
really know the consequences of their action, but because the
act is medically and ethically appropriate even though the
result—the patient's death—is both foreseeable and intended.
It commonly takes the form of putting a patient on an
intravenous morphine drip, with full knowledge that, while such
treatment will alleviate his pain, it will also indubitably hasten
his death. Analgesics, most notably morphine, when applied in
sufficient doses, will bring about a patient's death because they
serve to repress respiration. There can be no doubt, therefore,
that the actual cause of the patient's death is the drug
administered by the physician or by a person acting under his
supervision or direction.

The American Medical Association devotes a considerable
portion of the amicus brief it filed in this case to arguing that
doctors who give medication with knowledge that it will have a
double effect, including hastening death, should not be deemed
to have violated Washington's assisted suicide law. The
organization struggles mightily, albeit unsuccessfully, to
distinguish for legal purposes between the administration of
medication for a dual and a single effect. Nevertheless, we
agree with the AMA's point—the administration of dual effect

medication, with informed consent, does not constitute a criminal act. However, if, as the AMA contends, administering medicine that will result in death is lawful, we cannot comprehend the logic of its equivocal conclusion that prescribing life-ending medication for the patient at his request can constitute a crime, at least "at this time." (If the patient's consent has not been obtained for dual effect treatment, there would of course be even less justification for the AMA's fallacious distinction.) The line the AMA seeks to draw conflicts with reason as well as with the proper constitutional approach. The key factor in both dual effect and physician-assisted suicide cases is that it is the terminally ill patient's voluntary and informed wish that the doctor assist him to die through medical treatment. Were we to agree with those who would label some of the current medical practices engaged in at life's end as killing a patient or "euthanasia," we would put the AMA-sanctioned dual effect practice on that side of the line long before we would include the act of prescribing medication that is to be self-administered. It is the glaring inconsistency in the AMA's position that is undoubtedly responsible in part for the dissent's rejection of the AMA's plea to hold lawful the "dual effect" practice.

More specifically, we see little, if any, difference for constitutional or ethical purposes between providing medication with a double effect and providing medication with a single effect, as long as one of the known effects in each case is to hasten the end of the patient's life. Similarly, we see no ethical or constitutionally cognizable difference between a doctor pulling the plug on a respirator and his prescribing drugs which will permit a terminally ill patient to end his own life. In fact, some might argue that pulling the plug is a more culpable and aggressive act on the doctor's part and provides more reason for criminal prosecution. To us, what matters most is that the death of the patient is the intended result as surely in one case as in the other. In sum, we find the state's interests in preventing suicide do not make its interests substantially stronger here than in cases involving other forms of death-hastening medical intervention. To the extent that a difference exists, we conclude that it is one of degree and not of kind.

2.10) Withholding treatment is okay, but isn't aid-in-dying wrong?

This argument is also expressed as the "active versus passive euthanasia" argument.

Judge Reinhardt of the Ninth Circuit Court of Appeals addressed the distinction between withholding treatment, "passive euthanasia," and physician aid-in-dying, "active euthanasia."

That distinction, however, quickly proved unworkable, and after a while, terminally ill patients were allowed to reject both extraordinary and ordinary treatment. For a while, rejection of treatment, often through "do not resuscitate" orders, was permitted, but termination was not. This dividing line, which rested on the illusory distinction between commission and omission (or active and passive), also appeared for a short time to offer a natural point of repose for doctors, patients and the law. However, it, too, quickly proved untenable, and ultimately patients were allowed both to refuse and to terminate medical treatment, ordinary as well as extraordinary. Today, many states also allow the terminally ill to order their physicians to discontinue not just traditional medical treatment but the artificial provision of life-sustaining food and water, thus permitting the patients to die by self-starvation. Equally important, today doctors are generally permitted to administer death-inducing medication, as long as they can point to a concomitant pain-relieving purpose.

The distinctions suggested by the state do not individually or collectively serve to distinguish the medical practices society currently accepts. The first distinction—the line between commission and omission—is a distinction without a difference now that patients are permitted not only to decline all medical treatment, but to instruct their doctors to terminate whatever treatment, artificial or otherwise, they are receiving. In disconnecting a respirator, or authorizing its disconnection, a doctor is unquestionably committing an act; he is taking an active role in bringing about the patient's death. In fact, there can be no doubt that in such instances the doctor intends that, as the result of his action, the patient will die an earlier death than he otherwise would.

Similarly, drawing a distinction on the basis of whether the patient's death results from an underlying disease no longer has any legitimacy. While the distinction may once have seemed tenable, at least from a metaphysical standpoint, it was not based on a valid or practical legal foundation and was therefore quickly abandoned. When Nancy Cruzan's feeding and hydration tube was removed, she did not die of an underlying disease. Rather, she was allowed to starve to death. In fact, Ms. Cruzan was not even terminally ill at the time, but had a life expectancy of 30 years.

On April 2, 1996 Judge Roger J. Miner of the Second Circuit Court of Appeals argued that the abstract distinction between "active" versus "passive" suicide doesn't hold up in reality.

[T]here is nothing "natural" about causing death by means other than the original illness or its complications.

The withdrawal of nutrition brings on death by starvation; the withdrawal of hydration brings on death by dehydration; and the withdrawal of ventilation brings on respiratory failure. By ordering the discontinuance of these artificial life-sustaining processes or refusing to accept them in the first place, a patient hastens his death by means that are not natural in any sense. It certainly cannot be said that the death that immediately ensues is the natural result of the progression of the disease or condition from which the patient suffers.

Moreover, the writing of a prescription to hasten death, after consultation with a patient, involves a far less active role for the physician than is required in bringing about death through asphyxiation, starvation, and/or dehydration.

Withdrawal of life support requires physicians or those acting at their direction physically to remove equipment and, often, to administer palliative drugs which may themselves contribute to death. The ending of life by these means is nothing more nor less than assisted suicide....

2.11) Might doctors mistake someone who isn't really terminally ill?

Yes, it is possible for a doctor to misdiagnose a terminal illness. Such cases are exceptional rarities. And yes, in rare cases, even a person correctly diagnosed as terminally ill can make a miraculous recovery. The possibility of error, no matter how remote, exists. A person rationally choosing physician aid-in-dying must be told that such rarities do occur. Rarities happen∴

Judge Miner, writing for the Second Circuit Court of Appeals, addressed this problem.

[I]t seems clear that most physicians would agree on the definition of "terminally ill," at least for the purpose of the relief that the plaintiffs seek. The plaintiffs seek to hasten death only where a patient is in the "final stages" of "terminal illness," and it seems even more certain that physicians would agree on when this condition occurs.

Physicians are accustomed to advising patients and their families in this regard and frequently do so when decisions are to be made regarding the furnishing or withdrawal of life-support systems. Again, New York may define that stage of illness with greater particularity, require the opinion of more than one physician or impose any other obligation upon patients and physicians who collaborate in hastening death.

2.12) Dr. Storey's Story.

Dr. Don Storey is a founding member of both Deaconess and Sacred Heart Ethics Committees in Spokane, Washington. During Washington's Death With Dignity campaign, the courageous Dr. Storey often ended his talks with this story.

You're driving down the highway when you see a semi crashed ahead. The driver's not killed but he can't get out. The cab's on fire. He is going to die, without doubt. There's no hope of rescue.

He asks you to shoot him. Would you?

Now let's suppose you're an Emergency Medical Technician and you could give him a lethal dose of morphine to "end the pain." Would you?

If you wouldn't give him the injection, would you stop a qualified professional from giving it?

If you wouldn't give the injection and wouldn't allow anyone else to give it, please consider, "What would you want if you were the guy in the truck?"

Section 3: PATIENT

3.01) I won't need aid-in-dying, will I?

About two million Americans die every year; nearly 85% of them in
an institution. Of those deaths, some 80% involve a decision by
someone to try to prolong life or to let it go. It is estimated that
around four of every five Americans will die of lingering, chronic
illness which cannot be cured but can be artificially prolonged.
Odds are not in your favor to die naturally at home.

Death is inevitable and so is change. You probably do not believe a
lot of the stuff you believed as a kid. Beliefs change. Mortality
does not. Someday you may be dying and either thankful that your
belief system allows you to hasten death or wishing that you had
worked out your belief system so you could. Those whose beliefs
are inalterably against hastening death need not afford themselves
the option.

3.02) I have a Living Will (or Do Not Resuscitate
orders) so aren't I safe?

Despite the right-to-die movement, doctors often are oblivious to
dying patients' wishes. Dr. William Knaus was co-director of a $28
million study reported in the November 1995 issue of The Journal
of the American Medical Association. The study was conducted in
two phases. The first phase, from 1989 to 1991, followed 4,300
terminally or incurably ill persons at five teaching hospitals
throughout the United States. Almost half of the patients died
within six months. A third of the patients did not want to be
resuscitated but fewer than half of their doctors knew it. A third of
the patients and families did not want to talk about end-of-life
decisions. When Do Not Resuscitate (DNR) orders were given,
they were usually written within two days of death. Half the
patients who died were in moderate or severe pain during their last
three days. Thirty-eight percent spent more than 10 days in

intensive care. "Physicians are acknowledging that their patients are dying, but only at the last moment," Dr. Knaus concluded.

The second phase of the study, from 1991 to 1994, tracked 4,800 patients. Half of them were given specially trained nurses who helped them talk with their physicians about their care. The doctors were given complete and exact information about their patients' needs. But, according to Dr. Knaus, "It didn't work." The informed doctors' behaviors were no different than the uninformed ones. Dying patients still spent just as many days in intensive care, in comas, on breathing machines, used just as many hospital resources, endured just as much pain, and were just as late getting DNR orders. "We're going to have to develop a better vision for living well while dying," Dr. Knaus concluded, adding that the average cost per patient who died was $10,000. One third of the families reported losing most or all of their savings. One fourth of the patients had Living Wills but they "didn't make any difference" reported Dr. Knaus, adding bluntly, "The system doesn't know when to stop."

In 1988, Edward Winter's wife of 55 years suffered a massive heart attack and was revived by electric shock. As a result, she sustained brain damage and died in agony a few months later. Ed, then 82, decided he would not want to be resuscitated should the same fate befall him—which it did.

Despite the DNR order written in Ed's chart, he too was revived by electric shock. Two days later he suffered a crippling stroke. Ed was partly paralyzed and largely confined to his bed in a nursing home, and although he could still speak, he could only utter a few words before he began to cry in despair. Ed sued St. Francis-St. George Hospital in Cincinnati for "saving his life" against his wishes. Ed Winters died in September 1990.

3.03) Would terminally ill persons opt to die too soon?

The only one to decide whether or not it's "too soon" is the person dying. No one else can make such a deeply personal choice for another.

By the time terminally ill persons decide to hasten death, they have been examined by a physician, most likely shared the situation with loved ones, most probably received treatment, have gone through the agonizing steps of problem-solving to reach their decision, and have made arrangements to control their dying. Going through these steps takes time. "Too soon" is relative to your point of view.

As it is now, terminally ill persons feel the pressure to arrange for and hasten death while they still have the mental and physical capabilities to complete the task. They cannot wait too long or they might lose their ability to make the decision and to physically get it done. They must time their death early enough to carry it out effectively. Once aid-in-dying becomes legal, these people will not have the pressure to get it done while they still can. This alleviates a great deal of worry, and as **Dying Well Network's** experience has shown, those clients who have arranged control over their death, actually live longer! So, in actuality, a twist happens: Those who prepare to die earlier and may end up living longer! Clients typically say something like, "Now that the monkey's off my back I can relax and I feel better." The period of extension has been from a few days to a few weeks. Controlling death and controlling life are anything but dissimilar.

Death With Dignity initiatives in Washington (Initiative 119), California (Proposition 161) and Oregon (Measure 16) included procedures a terminally ill person had to take before he or she qualified for hastening dying. The time it takes to complete these procedures assures that a terminally ill person does not die "too soon." Dr. Kevorkian asks persons repeatedly if they are sure they want to go through with it or if they'd like to put it off or not do it at all. Both **Dying Well Network** and Compassion in Dying insist on such safeguards to guard against impulsive decision making. The act of hastening death has been called the "forever decision" because it can't be taken back. Safeguards must assure it is a rational and well considered decision.

Oregon's Death With Dignity Act, passed by the voters on November 8, 1994, places a "waiting period" for physician aid-in-dying to prevent impulsive suicide. The Act requires,

> No less than fifteen days shall elapse between the patient's initial and oral request and the writing of a prescription under this Act. No less than 48 hours shall elapse between the patient's written request and the writing of a prescription under this Act.

A patient requesting physician aid-in-dying can always rescind the request at any time. Oregon's Measure 16 spells it out directly.

> A patient may rescind his or her request at any time and in any manner without regard to his or her mental state. No prescription for medication under this Act may be written without the attending physician offering the qualified patient an opportunity to rescind the request.

The right to choose one's own way is more important than the timing. The American Library Association has declared Victor Frankl's book, Man's Search for Meaning, one of the ten most important books of this generation. Victor Frankl was a Jewish psychiatrist imprisoned in a German extermination camp during World War II. He saw many prisoners die soon after "giving up" and yet others lived in the same conditions without giving up. What made the difference? Frankl wrote,

> We who lived in concentration camps can remember the men who walked through the huts comforting others, giving away their last piece of bread. They may have been few in number, but they offered sufficient proof that everything can be taken from a person but one thing: The last of the human freedoms -

to choose one's attitude in any given set of circumstances, to choose one's own way.

The very last human freedom is to choose one's attitude toward death. One can choose to continue with treatment, to end treatment and begin comfort care with hospice or to end treatment and hasten one's own death at one's own time. One cannot exercise a choice if it is not available. The timing of the choice is not as important as having the choice.

3.04) If it were legal, would anyone ask for aid-in-dying?

One terminally ill woman, as she swallowed pills to hasten her death, stated simply, "Death isn't a punishment to avoid; it's a reward!"

A Roper poll of 1,982 people in March 1988 showed that 58% of those polled believed it should be lawful for a physician to lawfully end the life of a patient who requests it. Younger people, more so than older, thought it was acceptable. Professional people endorse it in greater numbers than do unskilled persons (64% to 57%). Different religious bodies have different attitudes toward assistance-in-dying. Many religions leave it to their members' individual conscience. The Roman Catholic church prohibits the choice, defining it as a "mortal sin." Fifty-five percent of the Protestants, and 69% of Jewish faith endorsed it. Among Roman Catholics a surprising 61% support physician assistance-in-dying even though their church's doctrine prohibits it. Only the Unitarian church has officially endorsed the right to die.

A February 1990 poll conducted by Time/CNN found that 81% of those polled believe if a patient is terminally ill and has left instructions in a living will, a doctor should be allowed to withdraw life-sustaining treatment. Fifty-seven percent believed it was all right for the physician to administer lethal injections or provide lethal pills. Polls taken since the 1970's show continually greater support for euthanasia and aid-in-dying. See professor Kearl's website <http://www.trinity.edu/~mkearl/death-5.html#eu> for graphic presentations of the changing public attitude. (Don't type the < > signs.) The graphs track opinions since the seventies across religiosity, education and concurrent beliefs on abortion and capital punishment.

Doctors Jack Kevorkian and Timothy Quill, Compassion In Dying, and **Dying Well Network** have helped terminally or incurably ill persons hasten death. There are no other known persons or organizations in the United States that have publicly admitted helping terminally ill people hasten death. There are many persons who have helped loved ones die in secret. The list includes Mary Tyler More. Two excellent and highly recommended books, Stephen Jamison's <u>Final Acts of Love</u> and Lonny Shavelson's <u>A Chosen Death</u> describe such deathings.

Many people in Holland ask for assistance in dying and two to six thousand persons a year receive it. About two-thirds of the Dutch favor active euthanasia. This ratio is similar to what we have in the United States.

Actually, the opinion polls aren't as important as your own opinion. The real question is, "Might I someday need and want the option?"

3.05) Client self-determination in end-of-life decisions.

The National Association of Social Workers (NASW) has an official policy regarding "Client Self-determination in End-Of-Life Decisions." The 1993 NASW Delegate Assembly defined "physician-assisted suicide" as "a patient's ending his or her life with the means requested of and provided by a physician for that purpose." The policy states,

> [S]ocial workers should be free to participate or not participate in assisted-suicide matters or other discussions concerning end-of-life decisions depending on their own beliefs, attitudes, and value systems. If a social worker is unable to help with

decisions about assisted suicide or other end-of-life choices, he or she has a professional obligation to refer patients and their families to competent professionals who are available to address end-of-life issues. It is inappropriate for social workers to deliver, supply, or personally participate in the commission of an act of assisted suicide when acting in their professional role. Doing so may subject the social worker to criminal charges. If legally permissible, it is not inappropriate for a social worker to be present during an assisted suicide if the client requests the social worker's presence.

NASW encourages its chapters to

facilitate their membership's participation in local, state, and national committees, activities, and task forces concerning client self-determination and end-of-life decisions.

Wouldn't it be wondrous if other professional organizations like the American Psychological, Psychiatric or Medical Associations would take such a bold and necessary stance in service of quality patient care?

Actually they may in the foreseeable future. On December 10, 1996 the American Counseling Association with approximately fifty-five thousand members filed an amicus brief with the U. S. Supreme Court. The Washington State Psychological Association (WSPA) and other groups co-sponsored that same brief. The WSPA stated carefully,

While the existence of a constitutional right to die is a legal question beyond the special expertise of the WSPA, WSPA hopes to demonstrate that evaluative processes do exist for reliably assessing mental capacity, even for patients who are terminally ill, and even for patients who may contemplate suicide.

The friends of the court argued that mental health professionals,

> guided by ethical principles that include patient autonomy and
> self-determination balanced by legal norms and concern for the
> public...(can) assess whether or not a terminally ill patient who
> has requested assistance in hastening death is mentally
> competent and has made a reasoned, informed, and voluntary
> decision to seek such assistance.

Before the WSPA made this statement the Social Issues and Human
Rights committee of the WSPA had sent the following statement to
the Executive committee asking that it be used as the basis of an
amicus brief from the WSPA to the U. S. Supreme Court.

> The Social Issues and Human Rights Committee of the
> Washington Psychological Association makes the following
> statement based upon the Ethical Principles of Psychologists
> and Code of Conduct of the American Psychological
> Association:

> Psychologists accord appropriate respect to the fundamental
> rights of individuals to privacy, confidentiality, self-
> determination, and autonomy, mindful that legal and other
> obligations may lead to inconsistency and conflict with the
> exercise of these rights. When conflicts occur among
> psychologists' obligations or concerns, they attempt to resolve
> these conflicts and to perform their roles in a responsible
> fashion that avoids or minimizes harm. Psychologists are aware
> of their professional and scientific responsibility to the
> community and the society in which they work and live.

> They apply and make public their knowledge of psychology in
> order to contribute to human welfare. Psychologists are
> concerned about and work to mitigate the causes of human
> suffering. If psychologists' ethical responsibilities conflict with
> law, psychologists make known their commitment to the Ethics
> Code and take steps to resolve the conflict in a reasonable
> manner.

Advances in medical technology now make it possible to prolong dying with little or no hope of recovery or quality of life. Medical miracles can become medical nightmares. A terminally ill person has the right to die and to make choices about the time and manner of his or her dying that preserve dignity, autonomy, and personal freedom. Psychologists have a special responsibility to balance the autonomy of their clients with the safety of the public. The rights of the individual should not take precedence over the rights of the society in which the individual lives; nor should the safety of society take precedence over the rights of the individual. Therefore, the right to die must be balanced with the right of the public to insure its safety from abuse. Psychologists attempt to balance conflicts between these rights by offering ethical principles and codes of conduct to help individual psychologists who have terminally ill clients and are faced with balancing such dilemmas.

A key value for psychologists is client autonomy. Clients are helped by exploring their informed choices. Alternative options, possible blatant or subtle coercion, beliefs, cognitions, affect, and style need exploration. Possible effects on others, from individual reactions to societal desensitization, should be examined. Psychologists do not promote any particular method of controlling one's life or one's death. Psychologists help clients explore, ameliorate, cope with, or solve problems which deny personal control over matters of life or death. Factors such as pain, depression, dignity, tranquillity, finances, effectiveness or futility of care are especially important considerations. Psychologists should act as liaisons with other health care professionals, family members, and others. Psychologists help clients express concerns, preferences, and needs to their care-givers to insure that treatment is compatible with the client's will.

Psychologists encourage clients to involve significant others in their decisions concerning end-of-life issues. Psychologists offer to mediate differences between persons concerning end-of-life decisions.

Psychologists are available to survivors as requested to offer support as they go through the grieving process.

Psychologists should be well-informed about living wills, durable power of attorney for health care, advanced health care directives, and issues concerning end-of-life decisions. Psychologists should be informed concerning the current status of the right-to-die issue as it moves through legislative and judicial processes. Psychologists are available to legislative and judicial processes exploring issues concerning end-of-life decisions.

Psychologists limit their practice to those areas within which they have been trained. Therefore, psychologists shall educate themselves concerning end-of-life decisions before practicing in this area.

Psychologists are autonomous and free to refuse to become involved in end-of-life decisions depending upon their own beliefs and values. When a psychologist chooses not to become involved in offering therapeutic support in end-of-life decisions, he or she has a professional obligation to refer clients and their significant others to other competent professionals who are available to address these issues. Psychologists who are involved in end-of-life processes with clients should inform and counsel such clients concerning the safeguards involved in end-of-life decisions. Psychologists may aid in determining competency, absence of coercion, informing significant others, absence of mental illness, exploring treatment alternatives, and insuring that end-of-life decisions are made with full informed consent.

Psychologists are knowledgeable about possible abuses and report abuse to the proper authorities as required.

Psychologists protect clients from harmful intrusions from persons and systems. Confidentiality is honored and protected.

Psychologists are especially aware to protect clients from unwanted and unwarranted involuntary treatment. Psychologists do not allow other professionals to affix the diagnosis of mental disorder solely on the basis of meeting diagnostic criteria for the disorder. In particular, a terminally ill person shall not be diagnosed as having a Major Affective Disorder solely because he or she meets certain diagnostic criteria on the basis of the vegetative symptoms secondary to the terminal illness.

Psychologists should inform clients considering hastening death that they can choose to discontinue those plans at any time. Psychologists should be supportive of their clients' decisions to hasten death when those clients meet appropriate qualifications as determined by law and when the clients' decisions are rational and congruent with the clients' beliefs and values.

No psychologist shall use physical means to cause or aid in the death of a client. No psychologist shall administer medication or otherwise be the causative agent in hastening death. Psychologists shall be held accountable to both legal and professional standards while helping clients concerning end-of-life decisions. Psychologists may choose to give information and be present before and during the client's death process, if requested.

Psychologists should counsel those who will be present at the death concerning what each person's role is to be. Psychologists should help insure that the death process is carried out in a peaceful, humane, and dignified manner for the client and those in attendance.

When a psychologist finds himself or herself in an ethical quandary, he or she shall hold the client's well-being in the highest regard and shall consult with a professional peer regarding a considered course of action.

Psychologists encourage and support education and research into end-of-life decisions.

3.06) Why can't a dying person have as good a death as a murderer gets?

Paul Lukes' letter to the editor of Hemlock Society's March-April, 1996 "Timelines" described how his 86 year-old father failed his attempt to hasten his death. His "higher cortical functions" were irreversibly destroyed by the time he was taken to the hospital where he was placed on a ventilator. Paul wrote,

On the night of the sixth day after his attempt at willful departure, I took a solitary turn with him, as I knew final farewells were upon us. An ever enlarged puddle of blood had collected in his urine bag. His glazed, blood-shot eyes stared blankly ahead. He continued to gasp air through a mouth parched by days of dehydration. His body had begun its gruesomely efficient prioritized shut-down sequence. His feet were purple, with gangrene. After some hours of desperate crying to which I had become accustomed lately, I held his frigid hand and kissed his feverish forehead good-bye, leaving at least partly relieved in knowing his suffering would soon end.

As my mother, sister and I gathered at his bed the next morning, we were struck by his persistence. His shriveled body continued to gasp, and his wilted ears sagged down his head. Though hooked to a morphine line, his dosage was maintained below lethal, as the law prescribed. A few drops more would cease his gasps, ending his torture. The end was known, as it had been four days earlier. Not knowing the method, I pleaded with the nurse, who could not help without risking prosecution for murder.

The dying man had been born in Prague. He had escaped the Nazi
regime by fleeing with his family to the U. S. Paul continued the
story of his father's death.

> Never did he suffer under Nazi imprisonment as he did under
> this misguided law in a society with a claim to civility. At best,
> the law reflects a society's naive and desperate denial of death's
> inevitability, and is barbaric in effect, if not in intent. It
> somehow absolves us of responsibility, as we pretend to discern
> a moral superiority of water's removal from a helpless creature
> to the active administration of painless drugs. At worst, it may
> be the medical industry's method of efficiently siphoning tens of
> thousands of dollars from a person's final days, continuing to
> skyrocket insurance premiums. Should a law be proposed to
> allow execution of the worst child murderers amongst us by
> slow dehydration, while they are fed just enough morphine to
> keep us oblivious to their suffering, a justified outcry would rise
> about such a law's inhumanity. Yet we prescribe this fate upon
> our most beloved. And would those who argue that "pain
> builds character" prescribe such a death to "rehabilitate" the
> child murderer? No! Then why would anyone suggest that a
> loved one dying slowly and "naturally" is somehow "building
> character" by following the "higher spiritual path?" This may
> be some people's way to deny the awfulness of some ways of
> dying.

3.07) Would physician aid-in-dying void life insurance?

Life insurance companies have to honor policies after a "suicide" if
the policy holder had paid premiums for at least two years (one year
in Colorado).

Oregon's Death With Dignity Act, passed by Oregon voters in
1994, addresses this issue squarely and succinctly. It placed the
following legal safeguards:

The sale, procurement, or issuance of any life, health, or accident insurance or annuity policy or the rate charged for any policy shall not be conditioned upon or affected by the making or rescinding of a request, by a person, for medication to end his or her life in a humane and dignified manner. Neither shall a qualified patient's act of ingesting medication to end his or her life in a humane and dignified manner have an effect upon a life, health, or accident insurance or annuity policy.

Section 4: SAFEGUARDS

4.01) Would this put us on a "slippery slope"?

To live in a civilized culture we must constantly draw lines. We decide where to place these lines by weighing where the possibility of good outweighs the possibility of harm. Opponents argue that once physicians are allowed to hasten death, then catastrophic abuse will follow. It is foolhardy to assert that there are not risks involved with the Death with Dignity movement. That's why there are specific penalties for violation of the terms of such legislation. Bringing end-of-treatment and end-of-life decisions under the law will provide more, not less, protection for dying persons, physicians, and society.

Life itself is precariously poised on a "slippery slope." We cannot avoid life's "slippery slopes." They are unavoidable. So we provide laws as guidelines and safeguards to draw lines and to anchor us. Hikers and climbers sometimes cross steep, icy and snowy, slippery slopes. They rope together and draw a line of travel along the best but least risky route. They set anchors into the snow and ice to insure safety. When aid-in-dying is legalized, lines will be drawn between individual rights and public safety. Public laws will set legal anchors to insure against slides down the "slippery slope."

Death with Dignity legislation will take aid-in-dying out of the secrecy where now it is clandestinely done and will place it into the public forum where safeguards can be standardized and regulated. Legalized aid-in-dying will provide greater, not lesser, individual freedom and public safety.

Ninth Circuit Court of Appeals Judge Reinhardt addressed the "slippery slope" argument.

> Once we recognize a liberty interest in hastening one's death, the argument goes, that interest will sweep away all restrictions

in its wake. It will only be a matter of time, the argument continues, before courts will sanction putting people to death, not because they are desperately ill and want to die, but because they are deemed to pose an unjustifiable burden on society. The dissent cites the experience in the Netherlands, where physician-aid-in-dying is allowed in some circumstances, to buttress both its claims that physician-assisted suicide cannot be adequately regulated and that approval of that limited practice will inevitably lead to the administration of death-inducing drugs without the patient's consent. We note that the reports on relevant medical practices in the Netherlands are so mixed that it is difficult to draw any conclusions from them. [This is] known as the "slippery slope" argument or what one commentator has called the "thin edge of the wedge" argument. The opponents of assisted-suicide conjure up a parade of horribles and insist that the only way to halt the downward spiral is to stop it before it starts.

This same nihilistic argument can be offered against any constitutionally-protected right or interest. Both before and after women were found to have a right to have an abortion, critics contended that legalizing that medical procedure would lead to its widespread use as a substitute for other forms of birth control or as a means of racial genocide. Inflammatory contentions regarding ways in which the recognition of the right would lead to the ruination of the country did not, however, deter the Supreme Court from first recognizing and then two decades later reaffirming a constitutionally-protected liberty interest in terminating an unwanted pregnancy. In fact, the Court has never refused to recognize a substantive due process liberty right or interest merely because there were difficulties in determining when and how to limit its exercise or because others might someday attempt to use it improperly.

Recognition of any right creates the possibility of abuse. The slippery slope fears of Roe's opponents have, of course, not materialized. The legalization of abortion has not undermined our commitment to life generally; nor, as some predicted, has it led to widespread infanticide. Similarly, there is no reason to believe that legalizing assisted suicide will lead to the horrific consequences its opponents suggest.

The slippery slope argument also comes in a second and closely related form. This version of the argument states that a due process interest in hastening one's death, even if the exercise of that interest is initially limited to the terminally ill, will prove infinitely expansive because it will be impossible to define the term "terminally ill." The argument rests on two false premises. First it presupposes a need for greater precision than is required in constitutional law. Second, it assumes that the terms "terminal illness" or "terminal condition" cannot be defined, even though those terms have in fact been defined repeatedly. They have, for example, been defined in a model statute, "The Uniform Rights of the Terminally Ill Act."

Our conclusion that there is a liberty interest in determining the time and manner of one's death does not mean that there is a concomitant right to exercise that interest in all circumstances or to do so free from state regulation. To the contrary, we explicitly recognize that some prohibitory and regulatory state action is fully consistent with constitutional principles.

Actually, physician aid-in-dying already happens. It happens in secret, without official safeguards or regulation. When physician aid-in-dying becomes legal and regulated, the public will be safer, not less safe!

4.02) Will it lead to Nazi-like atrocities?

This is America, not Nazi Germany. This is a democracy, not a dictatorship. There is a vast difference between Nazi Germany's involuntary genocide and Death with Dignity's voluntary aid-in-dying. Our legal system is comprised of checks and balances which safeguard against abuse.

The request for hastening death lies only in the hands of the patient. No one can ask to hasten the death of another. Aid-in-dying can only be given to adult, terminally ill persons who request it. It is always voluntary, never involuntary.

4.03) Is tube feeding an unquestionable right of life or a medical treatment which can be withdrawn?

Opponents used to argue that "tube feeding" is an unquestionable right of life. They argued that food and water are vital necessities of life which must be provided to all members of a responsible society no matter their physical or financial condition. They argued that artificial nutrition and hydration were irrefutable basics rights rather than medical treatments which could be refused. Now only the most radical opponents still voice this argument. Let's look at the history of artificial nutrition and hydration.

Artificial nutrition and hydration ("tube feeding") are complicated medical procedures. They are not just mashing up food and infusing water. In the seventeenth century a massive cholera epidemic spread through northern Europe. Sir Thomas Latta, a physician in Edinburgh, Scotland, discovered he could save the lives of some cholera patients by administering salt solution intravenously through the hollow quill of a feather. This dramatic result did not lead to the widespread use of intravenous hydration because most patients so treated died of massive infection. Not until the discovery of bacteria in the late nineteenth century and the development of special techniques for the manufacture and safe storage of bottles of sterile salt solution in the late nineteenth century could artificial hydration be successfully used as a medical procedure, which it most certainly is.

Intravenous nutrition came along more recently. Glucose, which provides all of the calories in IV fluids, deteriorates during the usual sterilization process. Special techniques in the 1930's and 1940's finally solved the problem.

Last to be solved was the ability to provide the essential nutrient, protein. Protein itself is toxic when given intravenously. Hence, it was necessary to give the protein building blocks called amino acids. It was not until the 1960's and 1970's that Japanese chemists were finally able to manufacture amino acids of sufficient purity to be given intravenously, a tremendous technical achievement for which they were awarded the Nobel Prize.

Early tube feeding treatment usually resulted in severe cramps, vomiting and chronic diarrhea. Specially formulated artificial nutrients finally solved this problem, although cramps, vomiting and diarrhea still represent significant medical complications which require medical monitoring and, often, treatment.

Radical opponents still argue that providing food and water to patients who cannot feed themselves is not medical treatment and therefore should be administered whether the patient wants them or not. Laurence O'Connell, vice-president for Theology, Mission and Ethics of the Catholic Health Association, disagrees. "Food and water," O'Connell has said, "are no more basic than air, and people find it acceptable to remove a respirator." In 1980 the Roman Catholic Church declared that refusing treatment "is not equivalent to suicide: on the contrary, it should be considered as an acceptance of the human condition...or a desire not to impose excessive expenses on the family or community." Using their own argument against them, isn't the rational suicide of a terminally ill person such "an acceptance of the human condition...(and) a desire not to impose excessive expenses on the family or community"?

Nowhere in the United States is a physician accused of giving aid-in-dying when following a dying person's request to be withdrawn from artificial nutrition and hydration. Neither is such a request seen to be a plea for suicide.

4.04)   How much does life-sustaining medical care at the end of life cost?

First, most Americans do not want "life-sustaining" medical treatment at the end of life. They don't see it as sustaining life, but rather as prolonging dying.

About 50% of patients admitted to an Intensive Care Unit (ICU) on respirators are terminally ill. It costs about $16,500 a month to keep a person on a respirator in an ICU. Often this money is spent on obviously terminally ill patients with virtually no chance of recovery. Doctors Knaus and Wagner wrote in <u>Science</u>, "In many cases, intrusive and complicated machinery is wheeled in to keep vital signs going, to give treatment of no benefit and tremendous cost, depriving others of treatment while dignity disappears." Note too that when the machines are wheeled in, loved ones are often escorted out.

Modern medical miracles can and do become modern medical nightmares both for the person dying and for the loved ones watching.

Dr. Emanuel, writing in the <u>New England Journal of Medicine</u>, disagrees with common estimates that there could be a $55 billion to $109 billion savings in health care dollars by limiting medical care provided to patients when acutely medically ill. He estimates the savings to be only $18.1 billion or only about 3.3% of the national expense for health care.

In 1990, a New York judge ruled that a Long Island Nursing home, Grace Plaza, could not collect about two years worth of $172-a-day fees for tending a 63 year-old comatose woman whose husband wanted her feeding tube removed because he knew she would not have wanted to be kept alive by artificial means. This means hospitals in some states can no longer force their institutional wills on unwilling patients and then make them pay for it.

Prudential, the nation's largest insurance company, was one of the first insurance companies to begin a new plan that lets a terminally ill policyholder have the bulk of their life insurance proceeds before they die. The program is meant to help people cover the high cost of dying.

4.05) Shouldn't the State protect life by always preventing suicide?

Judge Reinhardt, writing the conclusion of the Ninth Circuit Court of Appeals, addressed the issue of the State's duty to prevent suicide.

> While the state has a legitimate interest in preventing suicides in general, that interest, like the state's interest in preserving life, is substantially diminished in the case of terminally ill, competent adults who wish to die. One of the heartaches of suicide is the senseless loss of a life ended prematurely. In the case of a terminally ill adult who ends his life in the final stages of an incurable and painful degenerative disease, in order to avoid debilitating pain and a humiliating death, the decision to commit suicide is not senseless, and death does not come too early.... While some people who contemplate suicide can be restored to a state of physical and mental well-being, terminally ill adults who wish to die can only be maintained in a debilitated and deteriorating state, unable to enjoy the presence of family or friends. Not only is the state's interest in preventing such individuals from hastening their deaths of comparatively little weight, but its insistence on frustrating their wishes seems cruel indeed. In addition to the state's purported interest in preventing suicide, it has an additional interest in preventing deaths that occur as a result of errors in medical or legal judgment. We acknowledge that it is sometimes impossible to predict with certainty the duration of a terminally ill patient's remaining existence, just as it is sometimes impossible to say for certain whether a borderline individual is or is not mentally competent. However, we believe that sufficient safeguards can and will be developed by the state and medical profession to

ensure that the possibility of error will ordinarily be remote. Finally, although life and death decisions are of the gravest order, should an error actually occur it is likely to benefit the individual by permitting a victim of unmanageable pain and suffering to end his life peacefully and with dignity at the time he deems most desirable. There is some evidence that the state's efforts to prohibit assisted suicide in hopes of deterring suicide is at least partially counter-productive. As a result of the state's ban, some terminally ill adults probably commit suicide although they otherwise might not have done so and others probably commit suicide sooner than they would have done so.

In his recent book, Judge Richard Posner suggests that "permitting physician-assisted suicide . . . [in] cases of physical incapacity might actually reduce the number of suicides and postpone the suicides that occur." Judge Posner concludes that assuring such individuals that they would be able to end their lives later if they wished to, even if they became totally physically incapacitated, would deter them from committing suicide now and would also give such people a renewed peace of mind. He says that some of those individuals would eventually commit suicide but others would decide never to do so.

The suicide of Nobel Prize winning physicist Percy Bridgman, recounted in one of the amicus briefs, graphically illustrates the point. Dr. Bridgman, 79, was in the final stages of cancer when he shot himself on August 20, 1961, leaving a suicide note that said: "It is not decent for society to make a man do this to himself. Probably this is the last day I will be able to do it myself."

For no matter now much weight we could legitimately afford the state's interest in preventing suicide, that weight, when combined with the weight we give all the other state's interests, is insufficient to outweigh the terminally ill individual's interest in deciding whether to end his agony and suffering by hastening the time of his death with medication prescribed by his physician. The individual's interest in making that vital decision is compelling indeed, for no decision is more painful, delicate, personal, important, or final than the decision how and when one's life shall end. If broad general state policies can be used to deprive a terminally ill individual of the right to make that choice, it is hard to envision where the exercise of arbitrary and intrusive power by the state can be halted.

Like Judge Reinhardt in the Ninth Circuit Court of Appeals, Judge Miner in the Second, concluded that the State has little or no responsibility to ban physician aid-in-dying for the sake of suicide prevention.

At oral argument and in its brief, the state's contention has been that its principal interest is in preserving the life of all its citizens at all times and under all conditions. But what interest can the state possibly have in requiring the prolongation of a life that is all but ended? Surely, the state's interest lessens as the potential for life diminishes. And what business is it of the state to require the continuation of agony when the result is imminent and inevitable?

What concern prompts the state to interfere with a mentally competent patient's "right to define [his] own concept of existence, of meaning, of the universe, and of the mystery of human life" [Planned Parenthood v. Casey, 112 S. Ct. 2791, 2807, 1992] when the patient seeks to have drugs prescribed to end life during the final stages of a terminal illness? The greatly reduced interest of the state in preserving life compels the answer to these questions: "None."

4.06) Are safeguards adequate?

Ninth Circuit Court of Appeals Judge Reinhardt advocated for strong safeguards.

State laws or regulations governing physician-assisted suicide are both necessary and desirable to ensure against errors and abuse, and to protect legitimate state interests. Any of several model statutes might serve as an example of how these legitimate and important concerns can be addressed effectively. See, for instance, the procedural safeguards included in Oregon's Death With Dignity Act or the Michigan Model Statute Supporting Aid-In-Dying, appended to the Final Report of the Michigan Commission on Death and Dying. By adopting appropriate, reasonable, and properly drawn common safeguards, Washington could ensure that people who choose to have their doctors prescribe lethal doses of medication are truly competent and meet all of the requisite standards. Without endorsing the constitutionality of any particular procedural safeguards, we note that the state might, for example, require: witnesses to ensure voluntariness; reasonable, though short, waiting periods to prevent rash decisions; second medical opinions to confirm a patient's terminal status and also to confirm that the patient has been receiving proper treatment, including adequate comfort care; psychological examinations to ensure that the patient is not suffering from momentary or treatable depression; reporting procedures that will aid in the avoidance of abuse.

While there is always room for error in any human endeavor, we believe that sufficient protections can and will be developed by the various states, with the assistance of the medical profession and health care industry, to ensure that the possibility of error will be remote. We do not expect that, in this nation, the development of appropriate statutes and regulations will be taken lightly by any of the interested parties, or that those charged with their enforcement will fail to perform their duties properly. The Court explicitly recognized that states did not have to refrain from acting, but rather could adopt appropriate regulations to further their legitimate interests.

4.07) Proposed and active safeguards.

On November 11, 1994, Oregon voters approved "Measure 16" entitled the "Death With Dignity Act." It contains many safeguards. Here are the safeguards which are the responsibility of the attending physician:

The attending physician shall:

1. Make the initial determination of whether the patient has a terminal disease, is capable, and has made the request voluntarily;

2. Inform the patient of his or her medical diagnosis; his or her prognosis; the potential risks associated with taking the medication to be prescribed; the probable result of taking the medication to be prescribed; and, the feasible alternatives, including, but not limited to, comfort care, hospice care and pain control;

3. Refer the patient to a consulting physician for medical confirmation of the diagnosis, and for the determination that the patient is capable and acting voluntarily;

4. Refer the patient for counseling, if appropriate;

5. Request that the patient notify next of kin;

6. Notify the patient that he or she has the opportunity to rescind the request at any time and in any manner, and offer the patient the opportunity to rescind at the end of the 15 day waiting period;

7. Verify, immediately prior to writing the prescription for medication under this Act, that the patient is making an informed decision;

8. Fulfill the medical record documentation requirements;

9. Ensure that all appropriate steps are carried out in accordance with this Act prior to writing a prescription for

medication to enable a qualified patient to end his or her life in a humane and dignified manner.

The Model State Act was drafted by Dr. Baron, Professor of Law at Boston College Law School, and a team of lawyers, physicians, academics and Hemlock Society members in Boston. It was published in the Harvard Journal on Legislation in 1996. It fits squarely within the constitutional protections for physician-assisted suicide afforded by the for the Ninth Circuit's Court of Appeals. The Model State Act lists the following safeguards for determining if a patient qualifies for physician aid-in-dying:

1. The patient is eighteen years of age or older.

2. The patient has a terminal illness.

3. The patient has made a request of the responsible physician to provide medical means of suicide, which request is not the result of a distortion of the patient's judgment due to clinical depression or any other mental illness.

4. The decision represents the patient's reasoned choice based on an understanding of the information that the responsible physician has provided to the patient concerning the patient's medical condition and medical options.

5. The decision has been made free of undue influence by any person; and has been repeated without self-contradiction by the patient on two separate occasions at least fourteen days apart, the last of which is no more than seventy-two hours before the responsible physician provides the patient with the medical means of suicide.

(Please see section 8.03 "Qualifications" for the safeguards used by **Dying Well Network** to qualify clients.)

4.08) Would the poor, handicapped or minorities be pressured to die?

Judge Reinhardt of the Ninth Circuit Court of Appeals addressed this improbable argument as follows:

> One of the majority's prime arguments is that the statute is necessary to protect "the poor and minorities from exploitation,"—in other words, to protect the disadvantaged from becoming the victims of assisted suicide. This rationale simply recycles one of the more disingenuous and fallacious arguments raised in opposition to the legalization of abortion. The argument there was that the poor and the minorities would either be persuaded to have too many abortions or would be forced to have them against their will. The fact is that the poor and the minorities have been disproportionately deprived of the opportunity to have abortions, not only because they cannot afford such operations, but because in numerous instances restrictive legislation, sponsored by those who oppose abortion rights, prohibits the use of public funds to pay for them. In fact, as with abortion, there is far more reason to raise the opposite concern. The concern that the poor and the minorities, who have historically received the least adequate health care, will not be afforded a fair opportunity to obtain the medical assistance to which they are entitled—the assistance that would allow them to end their lives with a measure of dignity. The argument that disadvantaged persons will receive more medical services than the remainder of the population in one, and only one, area—assisted suicide—is ludicrous on its face. So, too, is the argument that the poor and the minorities will rush to volunteer for physician-assisted suicide because of their inability to secure adequate medical treatment.

Our analysis is similar regarding the argument relating to the handicapped. Again, the opponents of physician-assisted suicide urge a variation of the discredited anti-abortion argument. Despite the dire predictions, the disabled were not pressured into seeking abortions. Nor is it likely that the disabled will be pressured into committing physician-assisted suicide. Organizations representing the physically impaired are sufficiently active politically and sufficiently vigilant that they would soon put a halt to any effort to employ assisted suicide in a manner that affected their clients unfairly. There are other more subtle concerns, however, advanced by some representatives of the physically impaired, including the fear that certain physical disabilities will erroneously be deemed to make life "valueless." While we recognize the legitimacy of these concerns, we also recognize that seriously impaired individuals will, along with non-impaired individuals, be the beneficiaries of the liberty interest asserted here—and that if they are not afforded the option to control their own fate, they like many others will be compelled, against their will, to endure unusual and protracted suffering. The resolution that would be best for all, of course, would be to ensure that the practice of assisted suicide is conducted fairly and well, and that adequate safeguards sufficient to avoid the feared abuses are adopted and enforced.

Washington's statute prohibiting assisted suicide has a drastic impact on the terminally ill. By prohibiting physician assistance, it bars what for many terminally ill patients is the only palatable, and only practical, way to end their lives. Physically frail, confined to wheelchairs or beds, many terminally ill patients do not have the means or ability to kill themselves in the multitude of ways that healthy individuals can. Often, for example, they cannot even secure the medication or devices they would need to carry out their wishes.

4.09) What constitutes being "fully informed"?

Oregon voters passed the "Death With Dignity Act" on November 11, 1994. It spells out what constitutes "informed consent" for a patient requesting aid-in-dying.

'Informed decision' means a decision by a qualified patient, to request and obtain a prescription to end his or her life in a humane and dignified manner, that is based on an appreciation of the relevant facts and after being fully informed by the attending physician of

(a) his or her medical diagnosis;
(b) his or her prognosis;
(c) the potential risks associated with taking the medication to be prescribed;
(d) the probable result of taking the medication to be prescribed;
(e) the feasible alternatives, including, but not limited to, comfort care, hospice care and pain control.

4.10) Might not greedy heirs coerce rich relatives?

Proposed aid-in-dying legislation has always contained very strong prohibitions against coercion. For example, here's the language from Washington's "Death With Dignity" initiative.

Any person who

1. falsifies or forges the directive or another,

2. willfully conceals or withholds personal knowledge or a revocation of a directive,

3. causes the withholding of life-sustaining procedures, or

4. gives aid-in-dying without meeting the safeguards specified in the initiative will be subjected to prosecution for first degree murder.

Ninth Circuit Court of Appeals Judge Reinhardt addressed the concern about coercion.

There is a far more serious concern...the fear that infirm, elderly persons will come under undue pressure to end their lives from callous, financially burdened, or self-interested relatives, or others who have influence over them. The risk of undue influence is real—and it exists today. Persons with a stake in the outcome may now pressure the terminally ill to reject or decline life-saving treatment or take other steps likely to hasten their demise. Surrogates may make unfeeling life and death decisions for their incompetent relatives. This concern deserves serious consideration, as it did when the decision was made some time ago to permit the termination of life-support systems and the withdrawal or withholding of other forms of medical treatment, and when it was decided to recognize living wills, durable powers of attorney, and the right of courts to appoint substitute decision-makers. While we do not minimize the concern, the temptation to exert undue pressure is ordinarily tempered to a substantial degree in the case of the terminally ill by the knowledge that the person will die shortly in any event. Given the possibility of undue influence that already exists, the recognition of the right to physician-assisted suicide would not increase that risk unduly. In fact, the direct involvement of an impartial and professional third party in the decision-making process would more likely provide an important safeguard against such abuse.

We also realize that terminally ill patients may well feel pressured to hasten their deaths, not because of improper conduct by their loved ones, but rather for an opposite reason—out of concern for the economic welfare of their loved ones. Faced with the prospect of astronomical medical bills, terminally ill patients might decide that it is better for them to die before their health care expenses consume the life savings they planned to leave for their families, or, worse yet, burden their families with debts they may never be able to satisfy. While state regulations can help ensure that patients do not make rash, uninformed, or ill considered decisions, we are reluctant to say that, in a society in which the costs of protracted health care can be so exorbitant, it is improper for competent, terminally ill adults to take the economic welfare of their families and loved ones into consideration.

Judge Miner, writing for the unanimous decision of the Second
Court of Appeals, also addressed the danger of coercion.

> "[P]sychological pressure" can be applied just as much upon the
> elderly and infirm to consent to withdrawal of life-sustaining
> equipment as to take drugs to hasten death. There is no clear
> indication that there has been any problem in regard to the
> former, and there should be none as to the latter. In any event,
> the state of New York may establish rules and procedures to
> assure that all choices are free of such pressures.

Strong, stiff penalties can be created to protect against coercion.
Oregon's "Death With Dignity Act" has dealt with this possibility
by listing "Liabilities" as follows:

1. A person who without authorization of the patient willfully
    alters or forges a request for medication or conceals or
    destroys a rescission of that request with the intent or effect
    of causing the patient's death shall be guilty of a Class A
    felony.

2. A person who coerces or exerts undue influence on a
    patient to request medication for the purpose of ending the
    patient's life, or to destroy a rescission of such a request,
    shall be guilty of a Class A felony.

3. Nothing in this Act limits further liability for civil damages
    resulting from other negligent conduct or intentional
    misconduct by any persons.

4. The penalties in this Act do not preclude criminal penalties
    applicable under other law for conduct which is inconsistent
    with the provisions of this Act.

A more outrageous greed is not from coercing heirs, but from the
medical system itself. Drs. Gary Lee and William Perry achieved
standing as plaintiffs in the injunction against Oregon's Measure 16
by arguing that they and other doctors would suffer a financial loss
if terminally ill persons ended their lives instead of continuing

treatment. Bluntly stated, the doctors would lose money if the patient chose to die. Once a patient is dead he or she no longer runs up a bill! Keeping the patient alive feeds the system.

Ivan Illich, an author having the same name as the dying bureaucrat in Tolstoy's famous story, wrote of this dynamic after moving to rural Mexico. When a hospital was constructed in a near-by area, peasant families went completely broke getting dying family members the "best of care" in the hospital rather than letting them die at home with loved ones at their side as had been done in the area for more than a century. Illich called this "medical imperialism." But the medical establishment is not deliberately malicious. Please do not ascribe to maliciousness that which is simply incompetence.

Bill Houf, Minister Emeritus of the Unitarian-Universalist Church of Spokane and a Ph.D. in physics, says, "It's time we took dying back away from the doctors; they've bungled it long enough!"

4.11) Would surviving loved ones suffer knowing how the loved one died?

An agonizing, painful and uncontrolled death is more uncomfortably remembered by survivors than a humane and gentle one.

Jim, a forty year old father and husband, was dying from AIDS. He was not a drug user. He had never "shot up." He had never cheated on his wife and three children, all under age ten. He had not had a blood transfusion. He was not gay nor had he engaged in any homosexual activities. He was a chef. The best he could figure was that he had caught AIDS from teaching others to cut vegetables! Cuts and nicks happen. He used to wipe drops of blood off the cutting board, telling his trainees "not to worry." Jim didn't want his kids "to remember me sick and mean and not able to do anything." He took an anti-emetic, 10 grams of Seconal, 120 mg of Procardia and two shots of whiskey. After ingesting his "last meal" he laid back within a few minutes and never moved again. He died very gently and peacefully about eight hours later. His kids came home from school before he died. They were told that "Daddy's dying now." They were curious and examined him up close. They were satisfied that Dad was "doing real good" and so they left to watch TV and play outside. At the very end they returned to the bed. Jim's wife was holding him when he died. The end was a very gentle expiration. The three kids and the family dog were also comfortably on the queen-sized bed. When Jim died so gently, peacefully, and humanely, all present were comfortable that he had been able to "die well." The youngest child actually crawled over Dad, showing no fear at all of the warm cadaver. He saw and felt that Dad was "okay" and kissed him "good-bye." Mom's favorite brother had flown up to be with her. He too was on the bed, holding his sister's hand. When a **Dying Well Network** volunteer checked with the family a few months after Jim's death, his wife reported that the memory of the death remains a gentle and peaceful one for all who were present. Jim had done his "work." He and his wife had talked with the kids and appropriate loved ones. Knowing when he'd die Jim had a "deadline" (he enjoyed pointing out this pun) and had done his "last work" completely and well. It is not true that hastening death deprives persons from the final, sacred work they need to do to obtain complete closure. Neither is it true that controlled death leaves "bad" memories if done right.

Ninth Circuit Court of Appeals Judge Reinhardt addressed the "suffering survivors" concern as follows:

> The state clearly has a legitimate interest in safeguarding the interests of innocent third parties such as minor children and other family members dependent on persons who wish to commit suicide. That state interest, however, is of almost negligible weight when the patient is terminally ill and his death is imminent and inevitable. The state cannot help a minor child or any other innocent third party by forcing a terminally ill

patient to die a more protracted and painful death. In fact, witnessing a loved one suffer a slow and agonizing death as a result of state compulsion is more likely to harm than further the interests of innocent third parties. According to its protocol, Compassion In Dying will not assist terminally ill patients unless the patient has obtained the approval of family members or others with whom the patient has a close personal relationship. While we do not reach Compassion In Dying's claim or consider the merits of the safeguards it has devised, we note that a similar requirement by the state would raise constitutional concerns. We in no way suggest, however, that a private organization is not free to adopt higher standards than the state is permitted to impose in order to advance its interests or those of its clients.

There is an additional burden on loved ones and family members that is often overlooked. Some terminally ill persons enlist their children, parents, or others who care for them deeply, in an agonizing, brutal and damaging endeavor, criminalized by the state, to end their pain and suffering. The loving and dedicated persons who agree to help—even if they are fortunate enough to avoid prosecution, and almost all are—will likely suffer pain and guilt for the rest of their lives. Those who decline to assist may always wonder whether they should have tried to save their parent or mate from enduring, unnecessary and protracted agony. This burden would be substantially alleviated if doctors were authorized to assist terminally ill persons to end their lives and to supervise and direct others in the implementation of that process.

4.12) Is "aid-in-dying" a deceptive phrase?

The entire process of education is to "lead away from" (Latin: "exducare") or get rid of old ways of thinking. Learning is a process of making ever more exact cognitive differentiations and coining words to denote those "new" entities or ideas. The Inuits

(Eskimos) have many words for snow causing them to see snow in
many different ways. Language transforms our perceptions of
reality, and, mutually, our language is dependent upon our
perceptions. We need new words to express new meanings and see
the world in a new light.

Those who are for physician assistance in dying are often accused
of "twisting words" to meet our needs. When the Washington's
Death with Dignity initiative was filed with the Secretary of State,
the Catholic Coalition of Seattle went to court to have the title
changed to "Decriminalizing Physician Homicide." They lost.
Some opponents have defined physician assistance in dying as
"strong, healthy physicians killing weak, sick patients." Now that's
really twisting words!

Judge Reinhardt of the Ninth Circuit Court of Appeals chose words
carefully.

> While some people refer to the liberty interest implicated in
> right-to-die cases as a liberty interest in committing suicide, we
> do not describe it that way. We use the broader and more
> accurate terms, "the right to die," "determining the time and
> manner of one's death," and "hastening one's death" for an
> important reason. The liberty interest we examine encompasses
> a whole range of acts that are generally not considered to
> constitute "suicide." Included within the liberty interest we
> examine, for example, the act of refusing or terminating
> unwanted medical treatment. As we discuss later...a competent
> adult has a liberty interest in refusing to be connected to a
> respirator or in being disconnected from one, even if he is
> terminally ill and cannot live without mechanical assistance.
> The law does not classify the death of a patient that results from
> the granting of his wish to decline or discontinue treatment as
> "suicide." Nor does the law label the acts of those who help the
> patient carry out that wish, whether by physically disconnecting
> the respirator or by removing an intravenous tube, as assistance
> in suicide. Accordingly, we believe that the broader terms—

"the right to die," "controlling the time and manner of one's death," and "hastening one's death"—more accurately describe the liberty interest at issue here. Moreover, as we discuss later, we have serious doubts that the terms "suicide" and "assisted suicide" are appropriate legal descriptions of the specific conduct at issue here.

Moreover, we are doubtful that deaths resulting from terminally ill patients taking medication prescribed by their doctors should be classified as "suicide." Certainly, we see little basis for such a classification when deaths that result from patients' decisions to terminate life support systems or to refuse life-sustaining food and water, for example, are not. We believe that there is a strong argument that a decision by a terminally ill patient to hasten by medical means a death that is already in process, should not be classified as suicide. Thus, notwithstanding the generally accepted use of the term "physician-assisted suicide," we have serious doubt that the state's interest in preventing suicide is even implicated in this case.

"Euthanasia" is a word of Greek origin which means "good death" (Greek: "eu-thanatos" or "good-death"). Believe it or not, there are many young people who think that "euthanasia" means just what it sounds like to them: "Youth in Asia"! The word euthanasia is not synonymous with aid-in-dying. In euthanasia the physician administers the cause of death. In physician aid-in-dying the dying person self-administers the doctor's prescription so the patient is the active cause of death. There is a better balance of power in physician aid-in-dying than in euthanasia and therefore less likelihood of abuse.

Some doctors who are opposed to aid-in-dying say that they, too, "aid-in-dying." But when they say it they mean that they help people with comfort (palliative) care but not with "physician suicide." They don't like the fact that aid-in-dying has come to have a special meaning and they don't want to be thought of as a doctor who will not give aid-in-dying.

4.13) Is physician aid-in-dying "mercy killing"?

Mercy-killing is the felonious taking of life by a family member or friend out of intent to end suffering. It is not to be confused with aid-in-dying requested by the patient and provided by a physician.

Judge Reinhardt, of the Ninth Circuit Court of Appeals, defined euthanasia as "the act or practice of painlessly putting to death persons suffering from incurable and distressing disease, as an act of mercy, but not at the person's request." Judge Reinhardt defined physician aid-in-dying as "the prescribing of medication by a physician for the purpose of enabling a patient to end his life." Notice that in euthanasia the doctor administers the cause of death; in physician aid-in-dying the patient administers the cause of death. The patient, not the doctor, is the final, active agent. This balances power back to the patient. The doctor can prescribe, but cannot "put to death." This further insures that it is the patient's will that death occur. The patient, not the doctor or anyone else, has the final say.

4.14) Isn't starving people to death cruel?

Some terminally ill persons want neither to wait for a "natural death" nor to ask for physician aid-in-dying. They wonder if they could die by "just stopping eating and drinking." The following information is included for them.

For all of history, until very recently, people have been dying without artificial nutrition and hydration. In a natural death, the terminally ill person does not want and even refuses food and all but sips of water. It is natural for the dying to refrain from ingesting food and water. It is unnatural to "force-feed" the dying.

In 1986 Belding Scribner, MD, Professor of Medicine at the University of Washington, inventor of long term artificial kidney treatment and consultant on nutrition and hydration, testified before the Washington state Senate about whether it is humane to withdraw hydration. He stated the following:

Withholding of hydration has to be considered in two parts: First, the withholding of salt water (normal saline) causes no pain and suffering of any kind. It takes weeks or months for significant salt depletion to develop and when it does, the effect is a gradual drop in blood pressure and eventually a painless death from severe low blood pressure.

Secondly, concerning withholding of plain water, here is where opponents conjure up images of the '49ers dying of thirst in Death Valley with horrible thirst, swollen tongues and cracked lips. The case is quite different for the comatose, terminally ill patient lying in bed usually in an air-conditioned environment. The condition of the mouth depends upon the oral hygiene provided by the nursing staff, not on the state of hydration. Thirst, if present, is very subtle and easily treated, where appropriate, with ice chips or sips of water. There is no other pain and suffering that occurs.

Judge Reinhardt of the Ninth Circuit Court of Appeals declared that some doctors, preferring to help a terminally or incurably ill person starve to death rather than to give them aid-in-dying, only fool themselves into thinking they're doing the more moral act.

Similarly, when a doctor provides a conscious patient with medication to ease his discomfort while he starves himself to death—a practice that is not only legal but has been urged as an alternative to assisted suicide—the patient does not die of any underlying ailment. To the contrary, the doctor is helping the patient end his life by providing medication that makes it possible for the patient to achieve suicide by starvation.

By the way, persons in an irreversible coma or persistent vegetative state are in deep coma. They have no sense of time and they do not feel pleasure or pain. They do not sense the withdrawal of artificial nutrition and hydration.

4.15) Does wanting suicide show incompetence?

No, it does not.

Adults are assumed to be competent unless it is proven in court that they are not. Mental incompetence is a legal determination that can only be made by a judge following testimony, usually by a mental health professional like a psychiatrist or a psychologist.

Some argue that "You'd really have to be incompetent not to think of hastening death if you were in unrelenting, untreatable pain!"

4.16) Is suicide always irrational and therefore wrong?

Persons who consider suicide are usually depressed, stressed out, overwhelmed, angry or mentally ill. Suicide is a permanent false "solution" to a temporary problem. If someone is considering suicide he or she should get into counseling and, if necessary, be placed in a hospital, even if it is an involuntary admission. When the crisis is over persons who intend to commit suicide are almost always grateful that they were prevented. People who have jumped off the Golden Gate bridge and survived report that, after they cleared the rail, they knew they had made a mistake.

To the contrary, persons who have asked to be allowed to die but have been "brought back" are likely to be extraordinarily disappointed and are very likely to make another attempt.

Irrational suicide connotes the killing of one's self done in the throes of a mental illness or impulsively during the immediacy of an overwhelming crisis. It is usually done alone and in secret. If a person divulges an intent or a plan to "commit" suicide, the community of loved ones, friends and professionals intercede by nearly any and all means to prevent the act from occurring. Although it is not a crime to attempt a suicide, civil, rather than criminal regulations impose significant restrictions on the suicidal person. These restrictions continue until the person no longer expresses suicidal intent or makes a contract, in apparent good faith, with a responsible person not to kill one's self. Persons contemplating an irrational suicide almost always lack self esteem. They rarely talk openly and directly with appropriate loved ones about their thinking and plan. Even if loved ones object, persons contemplating irrational suicide continue their plans contrary to the wishes of loved ones. Irrational suicide does not take place with the consensual support of a loving community. Irrational suicides are often very violent and may disregard the health and safety of others. Those who survive the death of a loved one to irrational suicide are usually distraught about the tragedy of a life that ended "so suddenly" or was "wasted." Rarely do surviving loved ones find comfort that the "completer" died well. Surviving loved ones often describe the completed irrational suicide as being done by a "confused," "angry" or "troubled" person who "committed" a suicide, just as if a crime were committed. The completer is remembered in terms of being "guilty" dead. Survivors are usually personally and socially embarrassed by the death. Irrational suicides act like a contagion for more irrational suicides. Persons who receive adequate treatment after a failed irrational attempt are most often grateful to those who prevented the act or "saved" them. Irrational suicide is contrary to all religious traditions. The last hope of the person committing an irrational suicide is to end living. Irrational suicide ends life.

Rational suicide, on the other hand, includes the act of a terminally or incurably ill person to hasten death. It is an enduring rather than impulsive desire. It is done in the absence of a mental illness by a competent adult. Rational suicide is not expressed in terms of killing one's self. The terminally or incurably ill person would not even be considering a suicide if it were not for the underlying disease destroying the quality of his or her life. In the face of a devastating terminal or incurable illness and the nightmarish treatments used to fight it, most rational persons would consider suicide an option. A person in such a situation would be rational to consider suicide and irrational not to. The decision to end life is experienced as ending dying or hastening death rather than as killing self. Persons contemplating a rational suicide maintain self esteem. They almost always share their thinking and plan with one or more appropriate loved ones. If loved ones object to their plan, persons considering rational suicide may delay or even defer their plans for the sake of the others. Rational suicide takes place with the consensual support of a loving community. Persons completing a rational suicide prefer non-violent means and are concerned for the comfort, health and safety of others, especially related survivors. Persons who fail a rational suicide usually make continuing attempts, if they can, until the act is successfully completed. Those who remain after the rational suicide of a loved one are usually grateful that the completer was able to die well. Surviving loved ones often describe the deceased as being a "brave" and "courageous" person who "overcame an insurmountable obstacle." The completer is remembered in terms of being "peaceful" dead. Survivors are often proud of what they and the deceased accomplished together in the performance of a rational suicide. Rational suicides teach survivors how precious life is and do not lead others to irrational suicide. Rational suicide is supported by some religious traditions. The last hope of the terminally or incurably ill person is to end dying. Rational suicide ends dying.

4.17) What if aid-in-dying doesn't work?

Sometimes it does not. Taking medications on your own, even if you are following a prescription given in books such as Final Exit or Departing Drugs can fail.

Even a physician may fail to hasten death with certainty. On December 1, 1988, a jury in St. Petersburg, Florida found Dr. Peter Rosier not guilty of murdering his terminally ill wife. Dr. Rosier gave his wife, Pat, what he thought would be a lethal overdose of a sedative but when that did not work he tried to end her life by injecting her with morphine. The morphine was not lethal either. After 12 hours, unbeknownst to Dr. Rosier, Pat's father, Vincent, suffocated her with a pillow. After Dr. Rosier's acquittal, the jury foreman reported that "No one at any time during the jury pollings said 'guilty' to any one of the charges." Vincent escaped prosecution by getting immunity for his testimony at Dr. Rosier's trial. Pat's father, Vincent, had no regret for having helped his daughter die.

Physician assistance-in-dying must be legalized so it can be carried out in a controlled setting to prevent such tragedies in the future.

Russel Ogden studied assisted suicides among persons with AIDS in Vancouver between 1990 and 1993 as his research project for a master's degree in criminal law at Simon Fraser University. Only half were successful. Desperately seeking death, persons finally resorted to suffocation with pillows, slitting wrists with razors, shooting with guns and other active, violent means.

Even when physicians are involved, like what happens now in the Netherlands, about 12% of the deathings involve undesirable complications or unintended effects as reported by Gerrit van der Wal, Medical Inspector of Health in North Holland.

Ninth Circuit Court of Appeals Judge Reinhardt addressed the concern that deathing might not work as planned.

> Miscalculation can be tragic. It can lead to an even more painful and lingering death. Alternatively, if the medication reduces respiration enough to restrict the flow of oxygen to the brain but not enough to cause death, it can result in the patient's falling into a comatose or vegetative state. Some terminally ill patients who try to kill themselves are unsuccessful, maiming instead of killing themselves, or they succeed only after subjecting themselves to needless, excruciating pain.

Please do not try to hasten your own death without expert help from people experienced in successfully hastening death. (Please see section 7.09, "Why involve **Dying Well Network**?"). If you have no other choice but to try it yourself, please consider using a backup. Experts, including the authors of both Final Exit and Departing Drugs, recommend using a plastic bag to insure death.

The Right to Die Society of Canada (RTDSC) developed a hand-made, customized, plastic "Exit Bag" available from RTDSC, PO Box 39018, Victoria, British Columbia, Canada, V8V 4X8. The cost is $30 (U. S.), including discrete, airmail shipping. Add $10 for the manual and $16 for the book, Departing Drugs.

4.18) Does depression make a person incompetent to choose to die?

Far too often "experts" fail to differentiate between grief and depression. Regrettably terminally ill persons, victims of devastating physical illness, meet diagnostic criteria listed in the Diagnostic and Statistical Manual of Mental Disorders, Fourth Edition (DSM IV) for a depression simply as a result of the physical symptoms they experience as part of their terminal illness. For example, the DSM IV lists the following characteristics as indicative of a Major Depressive Episode. Five or more of the following characteristics must be present:

1. Depressed mood most of the day, nearly every day, as indicated by either subjective report (e.g., feels sad or empty) or observation made by others (e.g., appears tearful);

2. Markedly diminished interest or pleasure in all, or almost all activities most of the day, nearly every day (as indicated by either subjective account or observation made by others);

3. Significant weight loss when not dieting or weight gain (e.g., a change of more than 15% of body weight in a month), or decrease or increase in appetite nearly every day;

4. Insomnia or hypersomnia nearly every day;

5. Psychomotor agitation or retardation nearly every day (observable by others, not merely subjective feelings of restlessness or being slowed down);

6. Fatigue or loss of energy nearly every day;

7. Feelings of worthlessness or excessive or inappropriate guilt (which may be delusional) nearly every day (not merely self-reproach or guilt about being sick);

8. Diminished ability to think or concentrate, or indecisiveness, nearly every day (either by subjective account or as observed by others);

9. Recurrent thoughts of death (not just fear of dying), recurrent suicidal ideation without a specific plan, or a suicidal attempt or a specific plan for committing suicide.

Notice that a grievously ill person who is not psychologically depressed may meet criteria 2, 3, 4, 5, 6, and 9, thus warranting the diagnosis of a mental illness, Major Depression, simply on the basis of being terminally ill.

The expert diagnostician must differentiate depression from grief. Grief is simply a reaction to loss, whether that loss has already occurred or is about to happen (anticipatory grief). A terminally ill person is losing everything from interpersonal relationships to Beethoven's Ninth Symphony!

The expert diagnostician is not a computer-like list-checker; he or she is a compassionate human taking into account all relevant environmental, situational, social and psychological variables. The major differentiating characteristic between depression and grief is self-esteem. A person in grief keeps a healthy self-esteem; a depressed person usually nearly never does. The diagnostician who does not differentiate between physical and psychological causation of depressive characteristics and who does not differentiate between the low self-esteem of a depressed person versus the solid self-esteem of a grieving person is in error.

Please note that those of us who espouse Death With Dignity do not support the "irrational" suicide of a depressed person. We make the proper differentiations. Opponents to rational suicide usually don't. Many who oppose physician involvement in hastening death deliberately fail to make proper diagnoses, hoping to document a mental illness and thereby question the competency of a terminally ill person to make health care decisions.

An elderly gentleman in Spokane, Washington decided to end his terminal illness by starving himself to death. He had informed his immediate family of his intentions. His family agreed. However, once his weight became frighteningly low the family brought him to a Roman Catholic hospital against his will. Because he was grievously ill he met the diagnostic criteria for a Major Depression so he was involuntarily committed to the psychiatric unit where he was intubated against his will. Because he pulled out the tube repeatedly, he was placed in soft restraints. He begged to be allowed to die. His plight brought considerable attention to his case. A Roman Catholic ethicist, vehemently against Death With Dignity, interviewed him and determined that he was not depressed and was mentally competent. He was discharged, not to home, but to Eastern State Hospital's Geropsychiatric Unit where he died. His survivors have to remember that he died in a state mental hospital among strangers instead of at home among loved ones.

Can a "depressed" person give an informed consent to physician aid-in-dying? Certainly a person in the throes of grief, misdiagnosed as depressed, can make health care decisions.

Can a person who is correctly diagnosed as experiencing a Major Depression be competent? Adults are assumed to be competent unless it is proven in court that they aren't. Mental incompetence is a legal determination which can be made only by a judge, following testimony by a mental health professional like a psychologist or a psychiatrist, neither of which can, on their own, declare a person incompetent. Courts usually find persons competent to make health care decisions unless there are incapacitating cognitive or emotional disabilities which markedly disrupt the person's rationality. Neither the existence of a Major Depression nor most other mental disorders automatically disqualifies competency.

Even if a terminally ill person suffers from some "significant cognitive decline," the person may still be found competent. Courts will ask such questions as, "Can the person understand and remember the relevant facts necessary to make the decision?" "Does the person understand his or her situation?" and "Does the person appreciate the consequences of his or her choice?" If the person has an adequate command of these factors then the person will likely be found competent.

Oregon's Measure 16 requires a physician to refer a patient who requests aid-in-dying to "counseling" if the physician believes the patient may be depressed or otherwise mentally compromised. "Counseling" means, in Measure 16,

> a consultation between a state licensed psychiatrist or psychologist and a patient for the purpose of determining whether the patient is suffering from a psychiatric or psychological disorder, or depression causing impaired judgment.

Oregon's Death With Dignity Act leaves no doubt about this safeguard.

> If in the opinion of the attending physician or the consulting physician a patient may be suffering from a psychiatric or psychological disorder, or depression causing impaired judgment, either physician shall refer the patient for counseling. No medication to end a patient's life in a humane and dignified manner shall be prescribed until the person performing the counseling determines that the person is not suffering from a psychiatric or psychological disorder, or depression causing impaired judgment.

4.19) Do doctors abuse the right to die policy in Holland?

Strident opponents often bring up Holland's euthanasia policy as an example of what we shouldn't let happen here. They claim that many deaths in Holland are done by physicians without a request from the patient. Is this true?

John Griffiths, on the Faculty of Law at the University of Groningen in the Netherlands, wrote a report entitled "The Regulation of Euthanasia and Related Medical Procedures That Shorten Life in the Netherlands." He reports results of a major study commissioned by the Dutch government to study "Medical Decisions concerning the End of Life (MDEL)." Almost 90% of all Dutch doctors are, in principle, willing to give euthanasia or supply aid-in-dying. Two-thirds of those unwilling would refer a patient who requested euthanasia or aid-in-dying to another doctor. Griffiths found that of the 128,786 people dying in Holland in 1990, 3,700 (2.87%) involved physician aid-in-dying. Likewise, responsible estimates of how many patients will choose physician aid-in-dying in the U. S. usually hover below the 3% mark. Unfortunately about eight-tenths of one percent of deaths in Holland are labeled as deaths "without requests." Most of the deaths "without requests" were deaths of persons who had made it known what they wanted, but had not made an officially appropriate request. Still, there are abuses in Holland. They raise concerns about balancing individual rights with public safety.

Dutch safeguards presently include the following areas:

1. The patient's request: The doctor must ensure that it is voluntary and informed;

2. The patient's situation: This must entail unbearable suffering with no prospect of improvement, although pain is not essential; a somatic illness and the terminal phase of the patient's illness may be required;

3. The decision-making process: The doctor must discuss the situation with another doctor, the patient's family and the nursing personnel;

4. The doctor's record-keeping: This must include a full written account of the case;

5. The reporting: A certificate of natural death must not be filed in the case of euthanasia; the doctor is required to report each case of euthanasia as such.

Doctors who do not follow "rules of careful practice" ("zorgvuldig-heidseisen") are prosecuted or subjected to disciplinary measures.

Judge Miner addressed this fear of abuse directly.

It is difficult to see how the relief the plaintiffs seek would lead to the abuses found in the Netherlands. Moreover, note should be taken of the fact that the Royal Dutch Medical Association recently adopted new guidelines for those physicians who choose to accede to the wishes of patients to hasten death. Under the new guidelines, patients must self-administer drugs whenever possible, and the physicians must obtain a second opinion from another physician who has no relationship with the requesting physician or his patient.

Safeguards are important. Legislators must pass laws and administrators must develop procedures to insure that such abuses do not happen here in the U. S.

Section 5: COURTS

5.01) Is hastening death illegal?

In Washington State, a law (RCW 9A.36.060) made it a class C
felony to "assist a suicide." The law simply stated, "A person is
guilty of promoting a suicide when he knowingly causes or aids
another to attempt suicide." A class C felony is punishable by five
years in jail, a $10,000 fine, and, if the person assisting is a
professional, the professional could lose his or her license or
certification.

Early in 1994, four physicians, three terminally ill persons and
Compassion in Dying, a nonprofit organization, dedicated to
counseling and assisting terminally ill persons to choose the timing
and method of their death, filed a lawsuit in U. S. District Court
challenging Washington's "assisted suicide" law as unconstitutional.
On May 3, 1994, Federal District Judge, Barbara Rothstein, issued
a ruling finding Washington's "assisted suicide" law
unconstitutional. The Attorney General of Washington appealed to
the U. S. Ninth Circuit Court of Appeals to have Judge Rothstein's
decision overturned.

On March 9, 1995, a three-member panel of the Court of Appeals
voted 2 to 1 to reverse Judge Rothstein's decision, thus upholding
Washington's law against promoting a suicide. One of the judges,
a Roman Catholic, was a former director of a national right to life
organization! Compassion in Dying, et. al., appealed to the Ninth
Circuit Court of Appeals to re-study the issue with a panel of
eleven justices instead of three. On March 6, 1996, an eleven-
member panel concluded, eight to three, that the U. S. Constitution
protects the "right to life" and struck down Washington's ban on
assisting a suicide. Judge Reinhardt wrote the majority conclusion.

   A competent, terminally ill adult, having lived nearly the full
   measure of his life, has a strong liberty interest in choosing a

dignified and humane death rather than being reduced at the end
of his existence to a child-like state of helplessness, diapered,
sedated, incompetent.

This decision affected similar laws throughout the entire jurisdiction
of Ninth Circuit Court of Appeals. Similar laws placing a blanket
ban on any assistance in suicide were thereby overthrown in
Hawaii, Alaska, Oregon, California, Nevada, Arizona, Idaho and
Montana.

On April 2, 1996, Judge Roger J. Miner, writing a unanimous
decision for the Second Circuit Court of Appeals striking down
New York's law banning doctors from giving aid-in-dying,
concluded that New York's law prohibiting assisting a suicide
violated the Constitution's Equal Protection guarantee. New York
law allowed physicians to disconnect terminally ill persons from
life-support, a medical procedure which helped them die, but it
didn't allow physicians to write a prescription for a conscious
person to help them die. Through the use of a Living Will
terminally ill persons could ask a physician for a medical procedure
to end their lives when they became incapable of voicing their
wishes verbally, but conscious terminally ill persons couldn't ask a
physician directly for a medical procedure to end their lives. Judge
Miner argued that the New York law therefore discriminated
against conscious terminally ill persons.

Besides affecting the New York ban on assisting the suicide of a
qualified, terminally ill person the Second Circuit Court of Appeals'
decision also struck down similar laws in Connecticut and Vermont
as well.

Even though both the liberal Ninth and the conservative Second
Circuit Courts had reached very similar conclusions, Washington's
Attorney General asked the remainder of the twenty-four judges of
the Ninth Court of Appeals to re-hear the suit for the third time.
The Ninth Circuit Court refused. Within hours of that refusal U. S.
Supreme Court Judge, Sandra Day O'Connor, issued a stay order

blocking physician aid-in-dying from becoming legal within the
Ninth and Second jurisdictions. Judge Sandra Day O'Connor,
exercising responsible caution, thereby gave both Washington and
New York's Attorney-Generals the chance to appeal the decision to
the U. S. Supreme Court. The cases were appealed. On October
1, 1996, the Court took up the issue. The court will hear oral
arguments in January and it is estimated that the Court will have a
decision by July 1997.

5.02) The right to die.

Judge Stephen Reinhardt, writing the opinion of the eight affirming
justices of the Ninth Circuit Court of Appeals, specified what
protections are included within the right to die.

> We hold that a liberty interest exists in the choice of how and
> when one dies, and that the provision of the Washington statute
> banning assisted suicide, as applied to competent, terminally ill
> adults who wish to hasten their deaths by obtaining medication
> prescribed by their doctors, violates the Due Process Clause.
> We would add that those whose services are essential to help
> the terminally ill patient obtain and take that medication and
> who act under the supervision or direction of a physician are
> necessarily covered by our ruling. That includes the pharmacist
> who fills the prescription; the health care worker who facilitates
> the process; the family member or loved one who opens the
> bottle, places the pills in the patient's hand, advises him how
> many pills to take, and provides the necessary tea, water or
> other liquids; or the persons who help the patient to his death
> bed and provide the love and comfort so essential to a peaceful
> death. We recognize that this decision is a most difficult and
> controversial one, and that it leaves unresolved a large number
> of equally troublesome issues that will require resolution in the
> years ahead.

> This case raises an extraordinarily important and difficult issue.
> It compels us to address questions to which there are no easy or

simple answers, at law or otherwise. It requires us to confront the most basic of human concerns—the mortality of self and loved ones—and to balance the interest in preserving human life against the desire to die peacefully and with dignity. People of good will can and do passionately disagree about the proper result, perhaps even more intensely than they part ways over the constitutionality of restricting a woman's right to have an abortion. Heated though the debate may be, we must determine whether and how the United States Constitution applies to the controversy before us, a controversy that may touch more people more profoundly than any other issue the courts will face in the foreseeable future. [Underlining, not in original, provides emphasis.]

We first conclude that there is a constitutionally-protected liberty interest in determining the time and manner of one's own death, an interest that must be weighed against the state's legitimate and countervailing interests, especially those that relate to the preservation of human life. After balancing the competing interests, we conclude by answering the narrow question before us: We hold that insofar as the Washington statute prohibits physicians from prescribing life-ending medication for use by terminally ill, competent adults who wish to hasten their own deaths, it violates the Due Process Clause of the Fourteenth Amendment.

Because of the extraordinary importance of this case, we decided to rehear it en banc. We now affirm the District Court's decision and clarify the scope of the relief. We hold that the "or aids" provision of Washington statute RCW 9A.36.060, as applied to the prescription of life-ending medication for use by terminally ill, competent adult patients who wish to hasten their deaths, violates the Due Process Clause of the Fourteenth Amendment. Accordingly, we need not resolve the question whether that provision, in conjunction with other Washington laws regulating the treatment of terminally ill patients, also violates the Equal Protection Clause.

These matters, involving the most intimate and personal choices a person may make in a lifetime, choices central to personal dignity and autonomy, are central to the liberty protected by the Fourteenth Amendment. At the heart of liberty is the right to define one's own concept of existence, of meaning, of the universe, and of the mystery of human life. Beliefs about these matters could not define the attributes of personhood were they formed under compulsion of the State.

Like the decision of whether or not to have an abortion, the decision how and when to die is one of "the most intimate and personal choices a person may make in a lifetime," a choice "central to personal dignity and autonomy." A competent terminally ill adult, having lived nearly the full measure of his life, has a strong liberty interest in choosing a dignified and humane death rather than being reduced at the end of his existence to a childlike state of helplessness, diapered, sedated, incontinent. How a person dies not only determines the nature of the final period of his existence, but in many cases, the enduring memories held by those who love him.

For such patients, wracked by pain and deprived of all pleasure, a state-enforced prohibition on hastening their deaths condemns them to unrelieved misery or torture. Surely, a person's decision whether to endure or avoid such an existence constitutes one of the most, if not the most, "intimate and personal choices a person may make in a life-time," a choice that is "central to personal dignity and autonomy." Surely such a decision implicates a most vital liberty interest.

On April 2, 1996, Judge Roger J. Miner, writing a unanimous decision for the Second Circuit Court of Appeals striking down New York's law banning doctors from giving aid-in-dying, argued that, most likely, a right to die rests within the Due Process protection of the U. S. Constitution.

> [It] seems clear that New York does not treat similarly circumstanced persons alike: those in the final stages of terminal illness who are on life-support systems are allowed to hasten their deaths by directing the removal of such systems; but those who are similarly situated, except for the previous attachment of life-sustaining equipment, are not allowed to hasten death by self-administering prescribed drugs....

Unlike the Ninth, the Second Court of Appeals deferred to the Supreme Court to decide if there be a "new and fundamental" right-to-die.

> We (the Second Circuit) are mindful of the admonition of the Supreme Court (which declared), "Nor are we inclined to take a more expansive view of our authority to discover new fundamental rights imbedded in the Due Process Clause. The Court is most vulnerable and comes nearest to illegitimacy when it deals with judge-made constitutional law having little or no cognizable roots in the language or design of the Constitution." The right to assisted suicide finds no cognizable basis in the Constitution's language or design, even in the very limited cases of those competent persons who, in the final stages of terminal illness, seek the right to hasten death. We therefore decline the plaintiff's invitation to identify a new fundamental right, in the absence of a clear direction from the Court whose precedents we are bound to follow.... Our position in the judicial hierarchy constrains us to even more reluctance than the Court to undertake an expansive approach in this uncharted area.

A terrible fact remains about whether or not there is a "right to die": Terminally and incurably ill persons don't have an alternative to death. The only "rights" or choices they have are about the method, timing, and situation of their inevitable death.

5.03) But the U. S. Constitution doesn't mention a "right to die."

Absolutists are prone to make this argument. Absolutists believe there is an absolute Truth applicable to all people in all situations across all time. They tend to believe in literalist interpretations of the literature which they believe resulted from divine intervention or inspiration. They believe that every word of the Bible or the U. S. Constitution is divinely inspired and absolutely true for everyone even if they've never read either of the documents in entirety. Just as there are those who worship or make an idol of the Bible, "Bibliolatrists," there are those who nearly worship the U. S. Constitution, "Constitutionalists." They believe in a literalist, absolutist interpretation to which all people must subjugate themselves. (See section 7.08 "Hubris.")

Ninth Circuit Court of Appeals Judge Reinhardt explained how there can be a constitutional right when such a right is not even mentioned in the U. S. Constitution.

> The full scope of the liberty guaranteed by the Due Process Clause cannot be found in or limited by the precise terms of the specific guarantees elsewhere in the Constitution. This "liberty" is not a series of isolated points pricked out in terms of the taking of property; the freedom of speech, press, and religion; the right to keep and bear arms; the freedom from unreasonable searches and seizures; and so on. It is a rational continuum which, broadly speaking, includes a freedom from all substantial arbitrary impositions and purposeless restraints. . . . The makers of our Constitution undertook to secure conditions favorable to the pursuit of happiness. They recognized the significance of man's spiritual nature, of his feelings and of his intellect. They knew that only a part of the pain, pleasure and satisfaction of life are to be found in material things. They sought to protect Americans in their beliefs, their thoughts, their emotions and their sensations. They conferred, as against the

government, the right to be let alone—the most comprehensive of rights, and the right most valued by civilized men.

In deciding right-to-die cases, we are guided by the Court's approach to the abortion cases. Casey in particular provides a powerful precedent. . . . [T]he fundamental message of that case lies in its statements regarding the type of issue that confronts us here: "These matters, involving the most intimate and personal choices a person may make in a lifetime, choices central to personal dignity and autonomy, are central to the liberty protected by the Fourteenth Amendment."

In Casey, the Court made it clear that the fact that we have previously failed to acknowledge the existence of a particular liberty interest or even that we have previously prohibited its exercise is no barrier to recognizing its existence. . . . The Supreme Court did not directly address the constitutionality of proscriptions against interracial marriage until its decision in Loving. It could have done so previously but chose to sidestep the issue. At the time of the Loving decision, sixteen states still prohibited and punished interracial marriages. Six of those states went so far as to include in their state constitutions a provision banning interracial marriages. The Loving Court declared anti-miscegenation statutes unconstitutional, saying that they violated both the Equal Protection Clause and the Due Process Clause. In so doing, the Court rejected three hundred years of tradition and overwhelming precedent to the contrary.

5.04) Have the courts over-stepped their boundaries?

Judge Reinhardt of the Ninth Circuit Court of Appeals agreed that legislatures rather than the courts, should, if possible, decide such life and death matters.

To those who argue that courts should refrain from declaring that the terminally ill have a constitutional right to physician-assisted suicide and that we should leave such matters to the individual states, we reply that where important liberty interests are at stake it is not the proper role of the state to adopt statutes totally prohibiting their exercise. Rather, the state should enact regulatory measures that ensure that the exercise of those interests is properly circumscribed and that all necessary safeguards have been provided.

One problem with allowing each state to decide whether to prohibit the exercise of a liberty interest is the human suffering that results from a patchwork-quilt pattern of prohibitory legislation. Permitting assisted suicide in one state but prohibiting it in a neighboring one can easily lead to entangled legal battles in which the dying patient or his family tries to obtain approval for his transfer to the more permissive state. The unseemly legal struggle that ensues turns out all too often to have been academic, since by the time the matter is resolved, the patient has suffered the distressing fate he sought to avoid. The one remaining consequence of significance is easy to identify: Whatever the outcome here, a host of painful and agonizing issues involving the right to die will continue to confront the courts. More important, these problems will continue to plague growing numbers of Americans of advanced age as well as their families, dependents, and loved ones. The issue is truly one which deserves the most thorough, careful, and objective attention from all segments of society.

There is one final point we must emphasize. Some argue strongly that decisions regarding matters affecting life or death should not be made by the courts. Essentially, we agree with that proposition. In this case, by permitting the individual to exercise the right to choose we are following the constitutional mandate to take such decisions out of the hands of the government, both state and federal, and to put them where they rightly belong, in the hands of the people. We are allowing individuals to make the decisions that so profoundly affect their very existence—and precluding the state from intruding excessively into that critical realm. The Constitution and the courts stand as a bulwark between individual freedom and arbitrary and intrusive governmental power. Under our constitutional system, neither the state nor the majority of the people in a state can impose its will upon the individual in a matter so highly "central to personal dignity and autonomy."

As noted in the previous section, the Second Circuit court stopped short of declaring the existence of a "new, fundamental" right-to-die, deferring to the Supreme Court to make that decision.

5.05) At the Supreme Court.

On January 8, 1997, the U. S. Supreme Court heard two hours of legal arguments, one hour for Compassion in Dying v. State of Washington arising from the Ninth Circuit Court of Appeals, and one hour for Quill v. Vacco arising from the Second Circuit Court of Appeals. At issue was, simply, whether states may prohibit doctors from prescribing life-ending drugs for mentally competent but terminally ill persons who want to hasten death. Presently laws in 44 states make assisting a suicide a felony.

Thirty-eight groups filed friend-of-the-Court briefs against physician aid-in-dying and 16 filed briefs in favor of it.

Kathryn L. Tucker, representing plaintiff physicians from Washington, argued that the right to die arises from constitutional protection of bodily integrity, personal autonomy and a right to be free of unwanted pain and suffering. She stated, "These dying patients want a peaceful death; they want a humane death; they want a dignified death, and in order to access that kind of death they need the assistance of their physician."

Laurence H. Tribe, representing the doctors who challenged New York's ban on assisting suicide, argued against "terminal sedation." He said, "When facing imminent and inevitable death... (a terminally ill person should) not be forced by the government to endure a degree of pain and suffering that one can relieve only by being completely unconscious."

The justices expressed grave concerns about declaring that dying persons have a right to a doctor's help in hastening death, bringing up not only legal issues but also the role of modern medicine, evolving societal attitudes, moral considerations, and their own personal experiences around dying. The Court seemed to be concerned to avoid the vulnerability of declaring a right that society may have already embraced but not yet fully understood.

Justice Stephen G. Breyer said he was concerned that reports say "that only between 1 percent or 2 percent of all people need die in pain, but 25 percent or more do die in pain...." He wondered if "different groups, interacting with the legislature, are far more suited...to come up with an answer than a court writing a Constitutional provision?"

Justice Sandra Day O'Connor expressed concern about "whether it (the Court) should enter the balance of state interests versus the interests of the patient.... This is an issue that every one of us faces, young or old, male or female, whatever it might be. And all of us who are citizens and authorized to vote can certainly participate through that process in the development of state laws in this area." She also noted that if the Court finds a right to physician aid-in-dying that "It would result in a flow of cases through the court system for heaven knows how long."

Justice Ruth Bader Ginsburg, whose mother died of cervical cancer at age 47, observed, "Most of us have parents and other loved ones who have been through the dying process, and we've thought about these things." She noted and asked, "(When you) render a person unconscious, you withdraw the nutrition and water. It goes on for days and days and the person shrivels up and dies.... How is that rationally distinguishable from assisted suicide?" She also asked, "Isn't it possible that...a person could at one time, even for a period of days, say I want to die, I want to die, and didn't get the assistance, lives on, and says I'm glad that I didn't do that." She questioned, "You're talking about all these regulations.... Who is then to make these regulations?" She asked attorney Tucker why this issue couldn't be handled as a political matter to be debated and fine-tuned in state legislatures. Justice Ginsburg observed that "Everything you've said, it seems to me, could go on in a legislative chamber." Tucker replied that "Ours is a culture of denial of death" and terminally ill persons have no political advocates to represent them in legislatures. Attorney Tucker added that "This Court has never left to the legislative process the protection of vital liberties." Justice Ginsburg, a powerful women's rights advocate appointed by President Clinton, once said in a speech that she believed the Court had gone too far and too fast by declaring abortion a fundamental right.

Justice Anthony M. Kennedy, whose sister, Nancy, died of liver cancer in 1980, admonished the petitioning attorneys, "This is a question of ethics and of morals and of allocation of resources and of our commitment to treat the elderly and infirm and surely legislators have much more flexibility and a much greater capacity to absorb those kind of arguments and make those decisions than we do. You're asking us in effect to declare unconstitutional laws of fifty states."

Chief Justice William H. Rehnquist, whose wife, Natalie, died in 1991 after a long battle with ovarian cancer, forecast, "You're going to find the same thing I suspect that perhaps has happened with the abortion cases. There are people who are just totally opposed and people who are totally in favor of them. So you're going to have those factions fighting it out in every session of the legislature." He noted that the Court could be headed toward the legal and legislative turmoil like happened in 1973 when the Court declared the constitutional right to abortion in Roe v. Wade and then reaffirmed it in 1992.

Justice Antonin Scalia suggested his solution, "Why can't a society simply determine as a matter of public morality that it is wrong to

kill yourself just as it is wrong to kill someone else. What in the
Constitution prevents that moral judgment from being made in this
society's laws." Attorney Tribe explained that "When facing
imminent and inevitable death...(a person has the right) not to be
forced to be a creature of the state...(and to) have some voice...(in
the way)...the final chapter of life...(unfolds)." Justice Scalia
sarcastically interrupted, "This a lovely philosophy. Where is it in
the Constitution?" Justice Scalia asked attorney Tucker why
someone faced with ten years of "terrible suffering" rather than a
terminal illness shouldn't also have access to physician assisted
suicide. When attorney Tucker replied, "The dying process has
begun" for a terminally ill person. Justice Scalia blurted back, "I
have to tell you, the dying process of all of us has begun." In the
Fall of 1996, even though Justice Scalia knew the right to die issue
was approaching the Court, he announced to an assembly of
Catholic students that he finds "absolutely plain that there is no
right to die." On 11-11-96 TIME magazine accused him of
"prejudging the case on the high-court docket." Letters were sent
asking for Justice Scalia to recuse ("excuse") himself. He didn't.

Justice David H. Souter was concerned that "The risk is that the
practice of assistance is going to gravitate down to those who are
not terminally ill...out of physician assisted suicide into euthanasia."
He commented, "It may be impossible for a court to assess...until
there is more experience out in the world." He expressed a
sentiment similar to those of Justices Ginsburg, Breyer and
O'Connor, suggesting that "as an institution we are not in a
position to make the judgment now that you want us to make."
Justice Souter continued, "Twenty years ago we weren't even
reading about this. Maybe the Court should wait until it could
know more...before it passes ultimate judgment." Justice Ginsburg
then asked if it was merely a question of "just waiting." She
wondered aloud whether the Court should endorse physician
assisted suicide "now or ever." She added, "This case raises the
basic question of who decides. Is this ever a proper question for
courts to decide as opposed to legislators?"

Justice John Paul Stevens "sounded somewhat sympathetic to the arguments in favor of assisted suicide" according to a writer from the LA TIMES newspaper.

Justice Clarence Thomas asked no questions. His vote almost always is the same as Justice Rehnquist's and he aligns with Justice Scalia 92% of the time.

In the 1990 decision of Cruzan v. Director, Missouri Department of Health, the Court concluded that people have the "intimate and personal" right to avoid unwanted medical treatment by refusing artificial nutrition and hydration even if it means they will die. The Court concluded that the state could not intrude on the person's decision to end treatment because it was based on the right to be free of bodily interference or intrusion. The Court also stated in Cruzan that "legislatures should be allowed to resolve the issue without having their policy choices limited...(by the Court)."

If the Court declares a constitutional right to die then states cannot maintain their complete ban on physician aid-in-dying but could enact new laws to regulate it. If the Court declares that there is no such right then state legislators through law-making and state citizens through the initiative process could establish the right-to-die as Oregon voters did in 1994. There is presently an injunction against Oregon's Measure 16. It may be the next right to die issue placed before the Supreme Court.

The Court is unlikely to skirt the issue by using the "double effect" doctrine of the American Medical Association because it is contrary to the traditional legal concept that one is liable for results of actions which are probable though not overtly intentioned. Said more simply, the excuse that "I really didn't anticipate what usually happens" doesn't work.

The justices met two days later on Friday, 1-10-97, for a secret vote to find out where each stands. Their deliberations thereby begin. They will probably not announce their decision until the end of the term in late June or July.

The Justices of the Court seemed circumspect, maybe even outright wary, about declaring in favor of physician assistance in hastening death. They would affirm thereby an untested and, as yet, unregulated fundamental right. It would cause a great deal of extra work for the courts, for legislators and for administrators in both the public and private sectors.

While the Court was in session a bipartisan group of Congressmen, just across the street from the Supreme Court building, stated in a press conference that they intend to block any federal funds for doctor assisted suicide if the Court approves the right to die. Legislators have a past and present history of being intolerant to the idea of physician aid in dying. They are not likely to change soon. If the Court passes this issue to legislators, there is little hope for those terminally ill persons who seek to hasten death within the bounds of the law.

Parenthetically, no one mentioned Dr. Jack Kevorkian who has done so much to bring this issue to the public's attention. Dr. Kevorkian has helped about four dozen persons hasten death.

How long have Americans been reading about the right to die? In September 1895, the New York Times, covering the International Medico-Legal Congress, reported that a discussion "dropped into the extraordinary channel of the right of a physician to take the life of a man suffering from an incurable and painful malady." In reaction to this the February 1896 edition of Catholic World contained an article against euthanasia. Then in the July-December 1896 issue of the Overland Monthly Phil Weaver Jr., a travel and sports writer, wrote an 11-page science-fiction story entitled, "A Legal Suicide, 1996." In Weaver's prophetic story an attorney argues that his client, a man dying of stomach cancer and diagnosed as terminally ill by two physicians, had the Constitutional right to "exercise his liberty in (the) taking of…(his) mortal life…." Weaver's fictional attorney used exactly the same reasoning, the same argument, and offered one of the same safeguards as the real attorneys did almost exactly 100 years later! Wow!

Section 6: HISTORY

6.01) The case of Nancy Cruzan.

Nancy Cruzan was a 32 year old Missouri woman comatose for seven years after a car accident in 1983. Two state courts agreed that Nancy lay in a persistent vegetative state without cognitive brain function. In July 1988, a circuit court judge ruled that Nancy's parents, acting on her behalf, could order her feeding tube removed.

The attorney general of Missouri appealed the decision to the Missouri Supreme Court which reversed the trial judge, expressing belief that the state's interest in preserving Nancy's life outweighed her right to refuse treatment. The court ruled, "The state's interest in life is unqualified." The quality of life was, to that court, not germane.

The state of Missouri paid for Nancy's care. There are some 10,000 people now being kept alive in the U. S. in a persistent vegetative state.

Joyce and Lester Cruzan, Nancy's parents, then took Nancy's case to the U. S. Supreme Court. Supporting the Cruzan's petition to disconnect Nancy's feeding tube were the American Medical Association, the American Academy of Neurology, The American Nurses Association and the Society for the Right to Die. The American Academy of Neurology argued that "duty" requires doctors to continue treating unconscious patients as long as there is some chance of improvement. . .which Nancy didn't have. They concluded that when hope is gone, "duty ends."

On June 25, 1990, the United States Supreme Court, in a 5 to 4 vote, ruled that there was no "clear and convincing evidence" that proved Nancy would have wanted the tube feeding stopped despite the testimony and pleas of her parents, Lester and Joyce. Nancy, in her thirties, was predicted to "live" for another 30 years.

On December 14, 1990, the Curzans produced that "clear and convincing" evidence to Judge Charles Teel, Jr. The judge then ruled that Nancy Cruzan, in a permanent vegetative state since January 11, 1983, could be withdrawn from having chemical nutrition and hydration pumped into her stomach. She was expected to die within a week or so. The state of Missouri, which had opposed the removal of Cruzan's feeding tube, withdrew from the case after the Cruzans produced "clear evidence" that Nancy would have wanted to be taken off the tube feedings.

Nancy died Wednesday, December 26, 1990, twelve days after the tubes were removed. Lester and Joyce Cruzan, who had long held that their daughter was already "gone," issued a statement calling her "our bright flaming star who flew through the heavens of our lives."

After Nancy Cruzan had been taken off tube feeding, some religious bigots stormed the facility where Nancy lay dying. They were going to try to put her back on! They were stopped. Nineteen of them were placed in jail. A bigot is a person of strong conviction or prejudice, especially in matters of philosophy, politics, race or religion, who is intolerant of those who have differing opinions, no matter how reasonable or popular. Bigots cannot appreciate the valid opinions and beliefs of others. They will not follow democratic principles or even the laws of the land when they disagree with them. They follow their own absolute agenda which they dictate to all people across all situations across all time. They suffer from what Dr. Jack Kevorkian calls "a case of eternal ethics."

6.02) The case of Janet Adkins and Dr. Jack Kevorkian.

On June 4, 1990, Janet Adkins, a 54 year old woman with Alzheimer's disease, deliberately ended her life with the help of Dr. Jack Kevorkian, a retired pathologist in Michigan who had devised a way for a person to self administer a lethal dose of drugs to end life. Janet's husband and a friend of hers supported Janet's decision to end her life rather than, in Janet's words, "to put my family or myself through the agony of this terrible disease."

Janet Adkins was diagnosed as having Alzheimer's disease. Alzheimer's disease is an organic mental illness, a presenile dementia. Janet knew she was slowly and unrelentingly losing her mind. She may not have been mentally competent, especially in light of her diagnosis.

Alzheimer's disease is a terrible affliction which commonly lasts for years and only ends at death. Janet Adkins was not terminally ill; people don't die of Alzheimer's dementia. The question of competency arose.

KOMO TV, Channel Four in Seattle, focused on the Adkin's situation. Eighty percent of those who called in to cast their vote for or against Janet's "right to die" voted for it. We must exercise extreme caution to carefully consider what criteria are necessary to assure that terminally or incurably ill persons can receive physician assistance in dying.

Janet Adkins was Dr. Kevorkian's first patient. On December 13, 1990, Michigan District Judge Gerald McNally listened to a forty minute videotape made of Adkins and Dr. Kevorkian discussing Janet's fight against her Alzheimer's disease. "I've had enough," she said on the tape. Judge McNally then dismissed the first-degree murder charge against Dr. Jack Kevorkian, the 62 year old retired pathologist and inventor of the "suicide machine" Janet used to end her life. Janet's husband, Ronald, said he was relieved that the judge had dismissed the case, saying, "I and the family are very pleased and very grateful for the judge making the decision that he did."

Since then, Dr. Jack Kevorkian has gone on to help dozens of terminally or incurable patients die. He has been prosecuted repeatedly, but never convicted. "They can persecute and prosecute me, but they can't convict me," exclaimed Dr. Jack Kevorkian.

6.03) The case of "Diane" and Dr. Timothy Quill.

In March 7, 1991, the <u>New England Journal of Medicine</u> printed
Dr. Timothy Quill's article "Death and Dignity: A Case of
Individualized Decision Making." Dr. Quill is a licensed physician
working at the Genesee Hospital in Rochester, New York. He is
also a former director of a hospice program and therefore very
familiar with the treatment of dying patients.

"Diane" (a pseudonym) was a 45 year old patient Dr. Quill had
treated for eight years. She was raised in an alcoholic family, had
had vaginal cancer as a young woman, and had struggled much of
her adult life with depression and her own alcoholism. She
confronted her problems and gradually overcame them. She had
maintained complete abstinence from alcohol for more than three
years. Dr. Quill admired her strong sense of independence and
confidence. "She was an incredibly clear, at times brutally honest,
thinker and communicator," Dr. Quill wrote.

> Diane had been told by her oncologist (Cancer specialist) that
> she had acute myelomonocytic leukemia, a severe form of the
> disease that would end in her death within weeks or a few
> months without treatment. Treatment would consist of
> chemotherapy, irradiation, bone marrow transplantation and
> months of hospitalization. Diane was "enraged" when the
> oncologist presumed that she would want treatment and had
> begun plans to start chemotherapy that very afternoon. She
> refused treatment and went home. After two days of talking
> with her husband, her college age son, and her psychologist, she
> kept her decision to refuse treatment.

Dr. Quill talked repeatedly with Diane about her fear of a lingering
death or of the treatment which only had about a 25% chance of
giving her a cure. She said she wanted to "take her life in the least
painful way possible." Dr. Quill referred her to information
available from the Hemlock Society. Dr. Quill wrote the following:

A week later she phoned me with a request for barbiturates for sleep. Since I knew that this was an essential ingredient in a Hemlock Society suicide, I asked her to come to the office and talk things over. She was more than willing to protect me by participating in a superficial conversation about her insomnia, but it was important to me to know how she planned to use the drugs and to be sure that she was not in despair or overwhelmed in a way that might color her judgment. In our discussion, it was apparent that she was having trouble sleeping, but it was also evident that the security of having enough barbiturates available to commit suicide, when and if the time came, would leave her secure enough to live fully and concentrate on the present. It was clear that she was not despondent and that in fact she was making deep personal connections with her family and close friends. I made sure that she knew how to use the barbiturates for sleep, and also that she knew the amount needed to commit suicide. We agreed to meet regularly, and she promised to meet with me before taking her life, to ensure all other avenues had been exhausted. I wrote the prescription with an uneasy feeling about the boundaries I was exploring spiritual, legal, professional, and personal. Yet I also felt strongly that I was setting her free to get the most out of the time she had left, and to maintain dignity and control on her own terms until her death.

Diane lived "several very intense and important" months with her husband, son, and close friends.

[Then] it was clear the end was approaching. Diane's immediate future held what she feared most: increasing discomfort, dependence, and hard choices between pain and sedation. She called her closest friends and asked them to come over and say good-bye, telling them that she would be leaving soon.

She visited Dr. Quill for a last time. Two days after that visit, her husband called to tell Dr. Quill that Diane had died. Dr. Quill continued,

> She had said her final good-byes to her husband and son that morning, and asked them to leave her alone for an hour. After an hour, which must have seemed an eternity, they found her on the couch, lying very still and covered by her favorite shawl. There was no sign of struggle. She seemed to be at peace. I wonder whether the image of Diane's final aloneness will persist in the minds of her family, or if they will remember more the intense, meaningful months they had together before she died. I wonder whether Diane struggled in that last hour, and whether the Hemlock Society's way of death by suicide is the most benign. I wonder why Diane, who gave so much to so many of us, had to be alone for the last hour of her life.

Had Dr. Quill or Diane's family been with her they could have been charged with "aiding in a suicide," a felony crime at that time in New York where it happened, and in almost every other state.

Dr. Quill wrote his article because he had decided that it was important to tell the public and other doctors that it is right for doctors to help patients to maintain their dignity in dying.

The compassionate and courageous Dr. Quill was one of the physicians who sued the state of New York to overturn the state's blanket ban on assisting a suicide. That suit lead to the unanimous conclusions written by Judge Roger J. Miner of the Second Circuit Court of Appeals cited often in this book.

6.04) The case of Bertram Harper.

In August 1990, Bertram Harper, 73, his wife, Virginia, 69, and Virginia's daughter, Shanda, 40, traveled from Loomis, California to Detroit, Michigan where they believed it was not illegal to assist a suicide. Virginia was terminally ill with cancer. She wanted to die.

Virginia took pills and alcohol and placed a plastic bag over her head. The bag was uncomfortable so she took it off and put it back on three times in failed attempts to hasten her death. When she finally fell asleep Bertram put it on again and secured it with rubber bands. She died, cradled in Shanda's arms.

Bertram called the police. He was charged with manslaughter and offered probation with community service to be performed in California. Bertram rejected the offer insisting that he had not committed a crime. He went to trial and was acquitted.

"I knew in my heart that what I did was right," Bertram exclaimed. Shanda, who testified in her stepfather's defense added, "I just feel like he's been vindicated and my mother can rest in peace. We love her. We feel she made the right decision. We're glad we went with her."

Physician assistance in dying will prevent such tragic incidences. It will allow an act of hastening death to come out of secrecy. It will lead to more, not less, public safety for all concerned.

6.05) The cases of Reverend John Evans and Betty Drumheller.

On May 8, 1995, John Evans, a 78 year old retired Unitarian-Universalist (UU) minister, became the twenty-second person Dr. Jack Kevorkian helped to die.

John Evans was a 1949 graduate of Harvard Divinity School and was minister to UU congregations in Pennsylvania, Ohio, New Jersey, California, and Vermont. He also earned a Master's degree in Library Service. After World War II, he joined the American Peace Crusade and the effort to prevent nuclear war. In Pittsburgh in 1950, he helped to form a committee to support civil liberties, which was later designated a "communist front" organization by the U. S. Attorney General. During the McCarthy period, that designation drew the attention of government authorities and he was fired from his job as a librarian in Detroit in 1954. Rev. Evans was a draft counselor in Oakland, California during the Viet Nam war and later joined the effort to organize woodworkers in Vermont. He was active in the Sojourner Truth Organization, which was, at that time, a radical interracial group in Chicago. He was actively involved in social justice issues throughout his life.

Before Rev. John Evans died, he wrote two letters. The first was addressed to trustees of several local Unitarian congregations. The second was addressed to the press. He actually sent neither. Copies of his letters, typed on the day he died, were received by this author from Dr. Kevorkian's attorney.

Letter one:

> I am making this request of several local Unitarian churches, hoping to receive an affirmative reply while time remains and my sickness moves its course. I have terminal pulmonary fibrosis.

> UU churches have supported freedom of belief, opinion and speech. Now there is another freedom in need of support: freedom to choose the time, manner, and place of one's death. Unlike other issues or "causes" common in our churches, the right to die is not only a principle to be supported in general or somewhere else -- it is here, now.

> The finality of this act has a religious quality to it that William James called "solemn, serious, and tender." This, as well as the vindictive behavior shown by civil authorities in such matters, makes the occasion one of sanctuary.

> Without disturbing your schedule for use of your building, will you rent me space, or a room, for my physician-assisted suicide? No special preparation would be required.

> For some twenty years, as a minister, I served churches in the Unitarian-Universalist Association. Now I need to ask if the movement that I have called "home" has a place for me.

> Sincerely yours, John E. Evans.

Letter two:

To the Press:

It had been my intention to send the enclosed request to several local churches. There were two reasons for doing so: first, to spare my wife having my death occur at home; second, to give churches the opportunity to act on an important ethical issue that, sooner or later, they must face.

But we decided to use our home, and I was persuaded that to make this request of churches now might jeopardize the whole effort. My experience with churches gave me little reason to expect that one was immediately ready to offer this kind of sanctuary.

The question remains. When such a request is made of you, what will be your answer?

Sincerely yours, John E. Evans.

Early in 1995, **Dying Well Network** asked the Unitarian-Universalist Church of Spokane, Washington if they would consider offering sanctuary to a terminally or incurably ill person seeking a place to hasten death in the presence of loved ones.

The church board did not tell its members about this request for more than a year until June of 1996 when Betty Drumheller, beginning treatment for acute leukemia, asked the Spokane church for sanctuary. She wrote,

Could...(the) church consider providing me with sanctuary to discontinue treatment and take measures to die peacefully and with dignity should I choose this alternative?

I pray that your answer will be favorable as end of life choices should carry with them maximum opportunity for self-determination.

Those of us who want ceremony of friends, rather than total isolation, beg for such an opportunity. The guarantee against isolation would be a planned farewell ceremony. I don't want to die alone.

I humbly assert that what I face in the next few weeks can be eased with the knowledge of such an alternative in mind.

The church responded,

We now have a task force beginning to develop a process to assist the congregation in studying and developing action plans and/or positions on social issues. That process is not yet in place and the congregation has not had the opportunity to address the death with dignity issue in depth or the request for sanctuary for terminally ill persons. Though we cannot accommodate your request for physical sanctuary, we can offer you our support of your inherent worth and dignity during this phase of your life.

Prompted by our request, the Social Justice committee will discuss having a liaison with **Dying Well Network**. The Social Justice committee is committed to pursuing the issue you have presented. Please know that we are with you in spirit and hopeful that your recovery is complete.

Dear reader, if you want to exercise your freedom of religion, to have a sacred, protected place in your church for one of the greatest religious acts you will ever make, make your request very early. The experience of the Unitarian-Universalist Church of Spokane suggests other churches may have as great or greater difficulty.

Some proponents of the right to die argue that asking a church for sanctuary is counterproductive to the movement because it is simply "sensationalism." It isn't. No one involved in a deathing wants it "sensationalized" because it would jeopardize getting the deathing done and it would focus unwanted attention on those in attendance, thereby increasing their legal jeopardy.

Police can easily break the private property barrier to stop a
"suicide." Violating the church-state barrier would be much more
difficult. Public sentiment would at least inhibit, if not outrightly
prevent, police from interfering with a deathing held in a church as
a religious event. (Please see section 1.12, "Is hastening death anti-
religious?") Church sanctuary does not have to be bodily resistance
or a physical barricade. Sanctuary is a moral and religious
boundary more so than a physical one. The right to die lies as much
within the public freedom to worship as within the private right to
be let alone, the right to privacy. Deathing is, fundamentally, an act
protected by the right to practice one's religion.

6.06) The case of Bob Dent and Dr. Philip Nitschke.

On September 22, 1996, Bob Dent, a 66 year-old carpenter and ex-
pilot, was the first person in the history of the world to receive legal
physician aid-in-dying. His wife of twenty years, Judy, supported
his decision to die. Bob lived in the city of Darwin located within
the Northern Territory of Australia. That May, the Northern
Territory's Legislative Assembly barely passed the Terminally Ill
Act by a vote of 13 to 12. It became effective on July 1, 1996.
The Act enables a qualified terminally ill person to request a
physician to administer a lethal drug (euthanasia) or provide it for
self-administration (physician aid-in-dying).

Bob was diagnosed with prostate cancer in 1991. Both his testicles
had been removed. He was impotent, had lost 25 kilograms, wore
a catheter and a leg beg and required 24-hour care. He reported, "I
cannot even get a hug in case my ribs crack." He was taking 30
pills a day, not including morphine which had made him feel even
sicker.

Five psychiatrists had refused to certify that he was not suffering a
treatable clinical depression. Finally a nationally renowned
psychiatrist from Sydney flew in to evaluate him. Dr. John Ellard
reported that Bob was "an intelligent and sensitive man, fully aware
of all the issues concerning him and his illness" and that Bob was

not suffering from a depression even though he was physically very weak from his terminal illness and wanting to end his life.

Bob had found his new-found Buddhist beliefs to give him the solution to his suffering. He renounced greedy attachment to life. He learned that "man is born with death in his hand." He understood "the unity of life and the elimination of suffering" and believed hastening death was consistent with his beliefs. At the time of death Bob put Dr. Nitschke at ease by reminding him that this was "an act of love." After a simple lunch of a ham sandwich and a glass of stout, he told Dr. Nitschke, "You're here to do a job; let's get on with it."

Dr. Nitschke used a portable lap-top computer connected to a syringe to inject lethal drugs into Bob's arm. The computer program required Bob to answer three final questions, the last one being, "In 15 seconds you will receive a lethal injection and die. Do you wish to proceed? Yes/No." The program could be stopped at any time. Bob pressed "Yes" and died peacefully within minutes.

The day before he died, Bob dictated this edited "Open Letter to Federal Parliamentarians." Here's some of Bob's open letter:

> I have no wish for further experimentation by the palliative care people in their efforts to control my pain. My current program involves taking 30 tablets a day! For months I have been on a roller-coaster of pain made worse by the unwanted side effects of the drugs. Morphine causes constipation - laxatives taken work erratically, often resulting in loss of bowel control in the middle of the night. I have to have a rubber sheet on my bed, like a child who is not yet toilet-trained. Other drugs given to enhance the pain-relieving effects of the morphine have caused me to feel suicidal to the point that I would have blown my head off if I had had a gun.

> I can do little for myself. My red cells are decreased in number and deformed because of the cancer in the bone marrow. This anemia causes shortness of breath and fainting.

My own pain is made worse by watching my wife suffering as she cares for me; cleaning up after my "accidents" in the middle of the night, and watching my body fade away. If I were to keep a pet animal in the same condition I am in, I would be prosecuted. I have always been an active, outgoing person, and being unable to live a normal life causes much mental and psychological pain, which can never be relieved by medication.

I read with increasing horror newspaper stories of Kevin Andrew's attempt to overturn the most compassionate piece of legislation in the world. (Actually, my wife has to read the newspaper stories to me as I can longer focus my eyes.) If you disagree with voluntary euthanasia, then don't use it, but don't deny me the right to use it if and when I want to.

Sydney, Australia's Roman Catholic Archbishop Edward Clancy told a news conference,

I was, and still am, deeply ashamed that Australia should be the only country in the world to legalize the killing of an innocent person. Respect, reverence for human life is a cornerstone of our civilization. When that goes, our society begins to unravel.

Father Gino Cooncetti, a Vatican moral theologian close to Pope John Paul II said,

One remains stupefied and horrified by this shocking case of euthanasia that was requested and granted. No law of the state can justify euthanasia. This would mean the end of human civilization based on love and justice.

Opposition is intense. Kevin Andrews, who Bob begged "not to attempt to overturn the most compassionate piece of legislation in the world," has introduced to the Australian federal Parliament a bill to abolish the Act.

Addressing the entire situation, "THE AGE," a newspaper in Melbourne, ran an editorial that concluded,

Imperfect though it may be in some respects, the Northern Territory legislation should not be wantonly struck down. Those - including the Prime Minister, Mr. John Howard - who are inclined to support the proposed veto must explain their qualms in rational and compelling terms. Lofty rhetoric based on fear or fallacy will not convince Australians who regard their stance as cowardly or callous.

Section 7: Challenge

7.01) The Courage to Advocate for the Right to Die.

Frances Graves, 76, a Death With Dignity pioneer, wrote:

There is concern throughout the world over denial of human rights. The violations include imprisonment without trial, torture, killings, and discrimination against women, racial, religious and political groups.

A less recognized but also important violation is increasingly occurring in our freedom-loving country. We deny incurable patients the right to die with dignity and to hasten a lingering, painful dying. Individuals who have lived free lives, making their own personal decisions since childhood, are being denied this last choice.

This denial is not yet well recognized as being a violation of human rights. This may be because the motive is good. The general idea of preserving life is good, but carrying it to an extreme is not. Following one's religion is good, but imposing it on another is not. Another reason this violation is often not recognized is the gradual nature of the increasing power of medical technology to maintain a semblance of life longer and longer. We are so pleased with great medical advances that we overlook their misuse and their painful side effects.

If we value freedom, we will not allow medical "ethics," certain religious beliefs, or outdated, misapplied laws to become paternalistic dictators at the end of our lives.

We must work for legal recognition of the right to die, just as some of us have worked for other rights. Our ancestors sometimes risked or lost their lives fighting for freedom we now enjoy. They were misunderstood and maligned, as we will be, but that is the price of freedom.

Let's work hard to grant the last wish of the terminally ill: To die with dignity!

7.02) The "Secret Psychosis."

- All Men are Mortal.
- Socrates is a Man.
- Therefore, Socrates is Mortal.

- Thank God I'm not Socrates!

We have been so conditioned to worship youth and to avoid aging that we shield ourselves from observing death or even talking about it much. We have falsely come to believe that we can escape death by ignoring it. Yet we still sense deeply within our bodies that death is inevitable; it is inherited at birth, a kind of "birth defect"! We unconsciously want to believe that somehow we will live forever even though we know that living forever would not be good for us...or for mother earth. We avoid writing wills, planning our funerals and talking directly about our own death.

A psychosis is a condition in which the psychotic person changes external reality to fit internal needs. The psychotic person sees things as a reflection of inner turmoil rather than seeing things as they actually are. We are psychotic when we deny our own mortality. However, the denial of death is so common that we share the common belief that somehow we will not die! Since this delusion is so commonly shared we fail to realize it as a "secret psychosis." We share it much to our detriment. We cannot accept and control that which we will not acknowledge; we are at the mercy of that which we deny. We have made of death a monster when it is actually just the final stage of life.

It is hard to speak about death forthrightly but song writers do it eloquently. Kenny Rogers' song "The Gambler," says it well: "You got to know when to hold'em; know when to fold'em; know when to walk away; know when to run." Kenny adds another clinically astute observation: "You never count your money when you're sittin' at the table; there'll be time enough for countin' when the dealin's done." Kenny knew that when you get greedy and can't let go, it's because you're too caught up "countin'" what you've got. You "got to know" not only when to "take in" but also when to "let go." When you do not "let go" you'll maybe end up killing yourself slowly by your own greed. The gambler believed, "The best you can hope for is to die in your sleep." He did; he "broke even."

People have learned, almost automatically, not to fill a glass or cup clear up to the very top, trying to "have it all." Likewise, our cup of life need not be filled to the brim to give us satisfaction.

Buddhists know that "Greedy attachment is the root of all suffering." Our culture teaches us too much self interest, greed - a greed for life even beyond dignity.

We can learn to live by learning to accept our limitations. The words of another song, "Rose," remind us, "And the soul afraid of dying can never learn to live!" Our mortality is like the salt in salt water. We are mainly comprised of salt water. If we took the salt out, we could not live. To be human we need to accept our "salty" mortality!

7.03) The Feminine Aspect of Death.

We have been conditioned to conceptualize death as prototypically masculine. Death is powerful. It is in over-control. It cannot to be denied. It is the ultimate bogey-man, a phantom who will, inevitably, hunt you down, maim and kill you. Though death is almost always seen as masculine, it has a feminine aspect as well.

Nurses view patients dying differently than doctors do. Liaschenko and Davis report in the <u>Journal of Medical Philosophy</u> that nurses focus on the patients' suffering while doctors focus on a "cultural tradition of morality in which a universal standard always assumes precedence over the particularities of a situation." Nurses view

death as "the end of life." Physicians view death as "the enemy in
any circumstance." Nurses accent "care" while doctors accent
"cure." Doctors tend to be technology-centered while nurses are
person-centered. Doctors maintain "scientific objectivity" while
nurses are much more likely to practice "hands on" care. Doctors
tend to view suffering as a "problem to be solved, molded and
manipulated" while nurses view suffering as a "lived and shared
experience." In summary, the main distinguishing difference
between physicians and nurses is the difference between "the
absolutist and the contextualist ethical perspectives." As nurses
introduce a more feminine aspect to medicine, they foster the
feminine aspect of death. (See section 2.03 "Won't nurses or other
health providers end up giving aid-in-dying?")

A great paradigmatic shift is taking place. The masculine anchor in
Western civilization is sinking. The buoyancy of a more feminine
world-view lifts this culture to a new awareness. Men are more
likely than women to use logic as the means to an end of an ethical
problem. Women will more likely use communication as the means
to solve ethical dilemmas; they will "talk it over." Men are more
conceptual, using concepts to figure out ethical dilemmas. Women
are more contextual, using the data of the situation to figure them
out. Men emphasize fairness, rights and rules; women emphasize
responsibility, relationships and experience. Women, in general are
more concerned about not doing bad, not hurting others. Men, in
general are more concerned about doing good, doing what's
"right." Men confront. Women protect. May there continue to be
a feminization of medical care! For more insightful information on
these differences please read Carol Gilligan's book, In a Different
Voice. It is empirically based on results from the Harvard Project
on Women's Psychology and the Development of Girls.

Great truths often can best be expressed in myth. A myth is not the
literal truth, yet it contains the truth. The words of a myth can only
point to the meaning; they are not the meaning itself. But our

tongues must wrap around the infinite to make it finite so our minds can take hold and find comfort in the holding.

At depth, there are many great polarities which help to define existence: Self-other, love-hate, freedom-destiny, and male-female. These polarities are not just polar opposites; they each participate in the core of the other. They help define each other. They are mutual. These depth polarities help clarify the greatest and deepest of all the polarities, the polarity that rests within the ground of being, the polarity of being and non-being, the polarity of life and death.

Love, which can be well defined as "overcoming separateness" cannot exist without a separateness to overcome. The word "exist" itself is founded on the concept of "standing apart." In Greek "ex" means "from" and "ist" means "to be." So "exist" means "to be from" or "to stand alone or apart from or in comparison to something else." Everything is defined by what it is and what it is not. At the ground of being is non-being. Without non-being being cannot exist. Non-being forces being to express itself. Simply stated, "You can't have one without the other."

Likewise, without death there can be no life. Plants grow from dirt which is the residual of prior life. So life and death are not just consecutive, they are concurrent, intermingled. Without cells dying constantly in our body we cannot repair, heal and replace ourselves. The life span of a white cell in our blood is only 72 hours; a red cell, three months; a cell in the lining of the intestine, two weeks. If the constant deathing in our body could be heard, we would rumble all the time. Death-in-life vibrates, hums, at the core of our being. It hums all of the time. We cannot live without death. We can say, with good depth of truth, "Death gives us birth." This is one of the feminine aspects of death.

Seeing another feminine aspect in death, we can say, "Death is the mother of love." When we know a loved one is about to die, we love that person even more dearly, less for granted and much more desperately. When we, ourselves, are about to die, we listen carefully, poignantly and passionately to the last playing of our favorite song, our favorite reading, the sound of our loved one's voice. Could anything not mortal be so sweet?

Imagine a poet, walking alone along a dimly lighted street, sees, displayed in a brilliantly lighted jewelry store window, a flower, on a pedestal, encased in a solid ball of glass. "So beautiful!" he muses. "It is far better than I, because it will last forever. But it is stuck, trapped in eternity...dreadfully isolated. I wish it could break its bounds, share its fragrance and die, returning again to the soil as the gift of life from whence it came...like me!" And so, found by the poet in each of us, love is born in mutual mortality.

In the beginning there was nothing. There could have been sound or maybe a motion but there was no wind and no sea. A long, lonely cry came out of the center from where there was nothing. The spirit of the East, where someday the sun would rise, came to the center bringing hope for newness. The spirit of the South heard the long, lonely cry and came to the center bringing caring and warmth. The spirit of the West heard the cry and brought "letting-go" to ease the pain of the long, lonely cry. And the spirit of the North heard the cry and came to the center bringing courage in adversity. When the spirits came together, they met each other. They gave each other bodies and that is how us humans were born.

Non-being forces being to express itself. The soul afraid of dying can never learn to live. Death is integral to life. Death is the mother of love.

All this is myth.

Let me share with you another myth. A very long time ago there was a very powerful warrior who conquered all the city-states in a huge geographical area somewhere in the Middle East. He was proud to be the country's first king. Under his rule and guidance the country grew strong. State sponsored botanical gardens were situated throughout the land. The people and the environment flourished.

He had a son. The son learned much from wise teachers and able warriors. The king was pleased that he and his country could raise such a fine young man.

Then one day while the king was presiding over the Supreme Court his son burst into the chambers. Out of breath, the son bowed respectfully, and asked, "Father, your Honor, may I speak?"

"Yes, my son," the solemn but concerned judge-king replied.

"Father, today I was in the royal botanical garden studying the roses when I saw Death. He opened his arms to embrace me. I ran. I need to leave here now. May I take your horse to escape far away to Damascus?"

"My son, take my fastest steed. A compliment of my best warriors shall accompany you. Go in haste! God's speed!"

The son left. The father tried to return to the business of the court but he could not. He adjourned the session to reconvene on the morrow. He went directly to the rose garden. There he planned to face death himself and, if need be, offer himself in place of his son.

There in the garden, to the mighty king's dread and hope, was Death, admiring the roses. The father-king approached him. "Don't threaten my son!" he demanded.

"I didn't threaten your son," Death replied.

"He told me you opened your arms for him!" the father exclaimed.

"Oh, you've got it all wrong," Death said. "I wasn't trying to take him away. I was just raising my arms in surprise. I couldn't hardly believe he was still here because I have such an important meeting with him tonight in Damascus."

7.04) The Necessity of Ritual.

As it now stands, a person seeking to hasten death has many worries. An early-on worry is, "Will I be able to get the drugs I need to die?" Once a supply of deporting drugs is cached, the dying person feels relieved of a heavy burden and actually experiences new energy to enjoy what life is left. "Once you know you can control your dying you can live a little longer and little better, so dying well should actually be called dying well and living well," a 58 year old woman said a shortly before she died well after a deliberate overdose.

The circumstances surrounding her death were worrisome to her and to those present at her death. She was worried she might "be found out" or that it might "take too long." She wanted her death to be quick so as not to increase the window of jeopardy for those who stayed with her. She wanted to have a peaceful death not only for herself but also for the survivors as well. The secrecy and the pressure of time caused all to be anxious. Eight hours after she took her overdose, she awakened, disappointed that she had not died as she had so badly wanted. "I'll try again," she affirmed before being told to drink water, lie back, trust the process and let the medication do its work. Not until 16 hours after she began her deathing, did she die comfortably, peacefully, gratefully and well.

During the deathing she and those with her had to conscientiously control the anxiety inherent in the circumstances. Deliberate calmness prevailed. Each treated each other gently and thoughtfully, receiving as well as giving loving kindness.

Ritual is vitally important here. It introduces loving community. Knowing that there is a ritual sets a sacred tone to the deathing. Deathing is a sacred rite of passage done best within the structure of sacred ritual. A reading, or even a meaningful prayer, chosen for its substantive exposition of the sacredness of life and death, can begin a deathing well and sustain it to the end. A reading or a meaningful prayer can mark the end of the dying, facilitate the celebration of a death well done, and give permission to the survivors to grieve their own loss.

Ritual is not just a sign pointing to something else, it is a symbol which participates in that to which it points. It points to depth and is depth at the same time. It releases the finite to the infinite. A rite of passage is made, and made better, by ritual.

7.05) Wilderness in Democracy.

Wilderness shows us that death is an integral part of the cycle of life. Trees lean; snags stand starkly; and rotting downfall returns to the soil from which new life springs. Death is not the end of life; it is part of its very essence. A walk in an ancient forest, rightly called "old growth," renews our spirit as we sense the death-in-life element. Death is affirmed as an ancient and necessary part of life.

A carefully manicured park is not wilderness. Dangerous leaning trees and snags are cut down. Down-fall is cleared away. Dead flowers are plucked out and new ones replanted in their places. Death is hidden or whisked away. Death-in-life is denied.

Democracy has a wilderness element which we must value. Not everything will work out as we want it to. When we feel thorns, let us not forget blossoms. No matter what the immediate political and legal repercussions of our work, we can take pride in the public's blossoming awareness and its willingness to help people die well. Let us value wilderness in democracy as we value death-in-life. We must honor the democratic process and work within it even though it makes our task much more difficult and risky. We must accept our losses just as we accept our death. It is the only way to live life fully.

7.06) Death-shift.

The year 2000, the turn of the millennium, marks a great shift in time. Many predict a great shift in consciousness as well. Here's a part of it. The shift from fearing and trying to avoid death, to

seeing death as a natural consequence of life, is a great
paradigmatic shift. It is a shaking of the foundations. Greek
mythology tells us that when Prometheus stole fire from the gods
he was bound belly-up to a boulder and his viscera were eaten by
scavengers daily. Each night he regenerated, only to face the same
fate again the next day. That's how we die now, our spirits eaten
daily by dialysis, respiration, chemical and radiation therapies.
Modern medical miracles too often become modern, seemingly
never-ending, medical nightmares.

Fear of death leads us to a greedy attachment to life at all costs.
Like Darth Vadar in the Star Wars movies we hack away at our
bodies to avoid death and find at last that we have become
dehumanized and evil. We find redemption when we finally accept
our mortality and die.

Death-shift reintroduces the spiritual dimension beyond the
religious. All religions arise from an ineffable spirituality. The
death with dignity movement introduces a shift back to bedrock
spirituality and to a message central to all religions: There are no
resurrections without deaths. The acceptance of death is a
prerequisite to resurrection. Grace and joy based religions are
investigating and accepting the wisdom of the death with dignity
movement.

Who most resists death-shift? Those who stand the most to lose by
the death with dignity movement, the hierarchy of guilt-based
religions and those who have a vested financial interest in
prolonging out-of-control dying. The leadership of the Roman
Catholic Church and the American Medical Association have
contributed heavily and argued strongly against death-shift. But
there's still hope because most Roman Catholics and most younger,
practicing physicians endorse the right to die. Vested interests
cannot block this paradigmatic shift back to our roots in both life
and death. Taking away the fear of death robs guilt based religions
of their strangle-hold on our spirits. Guilt and shame based religions

fear and condemn spirituality while joy and grace based religions celebrate it.

Technology drives religion and is about to drive it again. Guttenberg's printing press gave the Bible to the masses and made the Protestant Reformation possible. The Church no longer controlled access to the "word of God." People made up their own minds after reading the primary source. Now the internet allows people to access world religions. On the internet a fundamentalist Christian can communicate directly with a fundamentalist Moslem, a Unitarian or even an advocate of the deification of Thor. An immense cross-fertilization is occurring. Religious dialogue thwarts parochialism. With dialogue small ideas shift to bigger ones.

From deep antiquity comes the saying, "Optimum philosophia et sapientia est comtemplatio de mortis." It is translated as, "The acceptance of mortality is the best and highest point in philosophy and wisdom."

This shift reintroduces the feminine aspect of death. The masculine aspect of death is the pervading myth of our culture. Death, as only masculine, takes control, cannot be denied and demands its way. Death, as feminine, is transformed. It is more experientially and relationally based. A person gone from "out there" is still alive "in here." Death teaches us to love a little more desperately, without taking relationships for granted. Death, as feminine, becomes the mother of love.

Death-shift reintroduces environmental grounding. Death-shift switches death as enemy to death as friend, from death as something to be avoided to death as a natural and necessary part of life. Death is a natural part, the final part, of life. Birth brings death. We and Earth live and die together. When we accept our unity with the earth, we let go of greedy attachment to our individual life. We all cannot, and must not try to live forever. It is not good for us, our loved ones or for spaceship Earth herself. There is no life without death. Few plants grow unless first a seed falls into the dirt, splits open, and rises to face the sun. There is no dirt lest a plant falls to the earth, splits open and allows the seed to phoenix-like arise from its demise. Life and death are not consecutive, they are concurrent. The environmental focus of death-shift is to relearn, wisely, the ancient biological rhythm of continuous birthing and deathing, of never-ending joy and sorrow.

7.07) The "Bow Tie" Void.

There are two types of voids: The annihilating void and the fertile void.

At times in our lives each of us have felt drawn to an unwanted, but inevitable end. Imagine it now. You're in a terrible squeeze. The further you go forward, the more you get squeezed down. It's like the left side of a bow tie. The walls on each side keep angling inward until they meet at a point, a singularity…like being sucked into an imaginary black hole. The further you get sucked into the void the more you get squeezed down until there's nothing left. There's no freedom of choice. There's just inevitability ahead. In the end, nothing is possible. It's like death. This is the annihilating void.

At times in our lives each of us have felt wonderfully expansive. Imagine it now. You let go of your ego. You let go of the subject-object split. You aren't really attached to anything and because you aren't attached you've got nothing to lose and everything to gain. It's like the right side of a bow tie. The walls on each side diverge to a grand expansiveness which allows you to expand limitlessly. All kinds of choices are open to you. There's just freedom ahead. Nearly everything is possible. It's like birth. This is the fertile void.

The annihilating and the fertile voids are connected.

Imagine you're a fetus in a womb. You begin to feel waves of contractions around you. You're being pushed inevitably toward a small pelvic opening which narrows down to a diameter smaller than your head. You feel your head being crushed. Your existence, as you know it, is ending. This is the annihilating void. But wait! Once through the opening you're being born! Nearly limitless horizons open before you. This is the fertile void.

The connection between the annihilating void and the fertile void, the knot at the center of the bow tie, is the birth canal. Yet, at the beginning of the journey to birth, you felt like you were dying. The knot at the center of the bow tie doesn't feel like birthing; it feels like deathing. Another name for the knot at the center of the bow tie is the death canal. It just depends on your point of view, how far into the process you are at the moment.

The connection between the left, annihilating void, and the right side of the bow tie, the fertile void, is the knot at the center. The knot at the center is either birthing or deathing, depending on how far you are through the process, depending on your point of view. Spin the bow tie around and it reverses. See it from the back side and it reverses. Birthing and deathing are very similar indeed.

Using religious language the concept behind the "bow tie" void can be expressed succinctly: There is no resurrection without a death.

Some physicists suggest that the cosmos is an organism. Our cosmos has a birth in creation, in the "big bang." Our cosmos moves; the great spiral arms of galaxies rotate; the planets spin. Our cosmos consumes; stars burn. Our cosmos may reproduce through "black holes" to possible "big bang" creations on "the other side." Our cosmos may die, collapsing back into itself in a final singularity, an Armageddon, an awesomely big "black hole."

And when each of us takes a turn in the annihilating void, we need to remember that just a little further on, the fertile void begins. And when we're in the fertile void, we may be wise to know that just a little further on, we'll again be in an annihilating void. It happens repeatedly throughout life. Often what looks only like annihilation becomes a beginning. Deathings and birthings are incredibly linked. The dance of life and death continues throughout all time.

We and the cosmos may live and die together. We and the cosmos may live and die forever. It is said that a death chant calms the chanter facing death and thereby increases the chance that the chanter will continue to live: "Earth and Sky, you and I, live and die together. Earth and Sky, you and I, live and die forever."

7.08) Death With Dignity on the Internet.

Here are some worthy places to visit on the internet. DeathNET is found at <http://www.islandnet.com/~deathnet/open.html>. (Don't type the < > signs; just type what's between them.) DeathNET's "SPEEDYfinder" is a good place to start surfing aid-in-dying. ERGO! (Euthanasia Research and Guidance Organization) can be accessed from the same address. It's full of all sorts of useful data, including the latest news items from around the world. A "must-visit" site is the Scottish Voluntary Euthanasia Society's homepage at <http://www.net link.co.uk/users/vess/index.html>. This site is great for doing research on the Death With Dignity movement.

John Hofsess, Executive Director of the Right to Die Society of Canada, posts the "Nothing But The News" Right To Die Mailing List. He daily posts articles collected from all over the world concerning the right to die movement. John sends these articles as private e-mail. To get these postings e-mail your request to <jh@rights.org>. When you get John's very valuable service please consider sending him a contribution to offset his expenses.

To read the complete texts of both the Ninth Circuit Court of Appeals decision in Compassion in Dying v. State of Washington and the Second Circuit Court of Appeals decision in Quill v. Vacco go to DeathNET's "LAST RIGHTS" Online Library. All available, relevant court decisions concerning the right to die movement around the world are kept current at this site.

To contact the author of Death With Dignity FAQs e-mail <Rob.Neils@ior.com>.

7.09) Dying Well Network and Compassion in Dying.

Dying Well Network is a nonprofit organization created to supply information to terminally ill persons and their families. If requested, **Dying Well Network** may also be present at the time of death. **Dying Well Network** actively supports the right of an adult, competent, terminally ill person to choose the time and method of his or her death, within the bounds of the law.

Acceptance of death often leads to an increased quality of the life the terminally ill person has remaining. A terminally ill person lives better knowing that he or she may gain control over the physical pain, the psychological agony and the financial devastation of dying. Terminally ill persons who have had control over their living expect to have control over their dying.

Dying Well Network and Compassion in Dying strongly recommend against do-it-yourself attempts. Please contact either organization for reliable, up-to-date information. Their addresses are as follows:

> **Dying Well Network**
> **PO Box 880**
> **Spokane, WA 99210-0880**
> **Phone (509) 926-2457**
>
> **Compassion in Dying**
> **PO Box 75295**
> **Seattle, WA 98125-0295**
> **Phone: (206) 624-2775**

Please consider giving a charitable contribution to either non-profit organization. It is tax deductible. Even small donations are deeply appreciated.

Ninth Circuit Court Judge Reinhardt declared a constitutionally guaranteed right to die, but he did not address the right of an organization like Compassion In Dying to provide assistance to those who exercise that right:

The District Court...did not address the claim asserted by
Compassion In Dying. Nor, correlatively, did it reach the claim
by the terminally ill patients that they had a right to receive
assistance from organizations such as Compassion In Dying.
The claims involving Compassion In Dying are not before us.
The district court suggested that it would reach those additional
claims at a later stage in the proceedings if Compassion In
Dying so desired.

7.10) Why involve Dying Well Network?

You control your deathing. Once you have the latest information
from **Dying Well Network**, you can do it by yourself or with just a
loved one present. Why involve **Dying Well Network**?

For three reasons: Your physician, your loved ones and yourself.

Your physician needs to know what qualifies you for aid-in-dying,
what safeguards are to be followed, what drugs have the best
chance of working most gently and effectively with the least
probability of failure. **Dying Well Network** has the latest
pharmaceutical information available. Your physician needs to
know that you are competent, that you are not being coerced, and
that your request is an enduring one, not impulsive nor arising from
a clinical depression. **Dying Well Network** has a clinical
structured interview to carefully differentiate a "rational" from an
"irrational" suicide. **Dying Well Network** informs the physician
that you have discussed your decision with appropriate loved ones,
that they agree with your decision and, if they don't, then **Dying
Well Network** will, if requested, mediate differences between
family members. **Dying Well Network** knows which pharmacists
are most willing to help and be discrete about it. **Dying Well
Network** can be at the deathing to offer expertise, guidance,
comfort and aid if anything goes wrong. Simply put, because
physicians are safer when their patients use **Dying Well Network,**
they are more likely not to refuse to write the needed prescription.

Loved ones, especially those who will be with you as you hasten your death, benefit from **Dying Well Network's** presence. **Dying Well Network** witnesses that you are the active agent of your death. **Dying Well Network**'s presence is especially needed for those who stand to benefit in any way by your death. **Dying Well Network** can assure that a caregiver didn't subtly coerce you to die so that they could get financial gain or be relieved of the difficult task of caring for you. If your loved ones are mentioned in your will, they are vulnerable to accusations that they helped you die for selfish or illegal reasons. **Dying Well Network** has experience in deathings and can help set a dignified and peaceful atmosphere at your deathing. **Dying Well Network** can offer suggestions like adding applesauce or a sweetener to the drugs you take so they are more palatable and go down easier. **Dying Well Network** can be there for you and your loved ones if anything goes wrong with your deathing.

Dying Well Network can review your situation and treatment history to be sure that there isn't a better alternative left to try. If your physician refuses your request **Dying Well Network** can refer you to a physician who may be willing to help. You can be assured that your death will go as gently and effectively as possible. **Dying Well Network** can offer guidance about how to prepare and take the prescription, what to ingest it with, and how long to wait between steps in the procedure. You can know with confidence that the procedure for your deathing will be effectively guided by persons who have helped at other deathings. **Dying Well Network** can help by listening for a heartbeat and checking for a pupil response to be sure that your death has actually occurred. **Dying Well Network** gives presence and protection to your loved ones so you don't have to worry about their comfort and safety.

Dying Well Network will be as most helpful and least intrusive as possible during the deathing. Dying Well personnel can wait within the home but not in the bedroom if so desired. **Dying Well Network** maintains strict confidentiality.

If you want to go through it alone, you can. If you decide not to have **Dying Well Network** present, you will need to talk with someone about what will be done in case of something going wrong. Loved ones, exhausted from a failing deathing have been known to call 911 in panic.

Quite often males, not terminally ill but considering the idea of physician aid-in-dying, blurt out rather impulsively, "What's to stop me from just taking a gun and blowing my brains out?" The answer is, starkly, "Nothing...if you're secret about it; if you don't consider the trauma you'll inflict on your body; and if you're not considerate of the person who finds you or has to clean up the mess."

Section 8: DYING WELL NETWORK

The data in this section is included in <u>Death With Dignity FAQs</u> for those who want to understand how the intricacies of aid-in-dying actually work out in real life.

8.01) Purpose

Dying Well Network is a nonprofit organization created to supply information to terminally ill persons and their families. If requested, **Dying Well Network** may also be present at the time of death. **Dying Well Network** actively supports the right of an adult, competent, terminally ill person to choose the time and method of his or her death, within the bounds of the law.

Acceptance of death often leads to an increased quality of the life the terminally ill person has remaining. A terminally ill person lives better knowing that he or she may gain control over the physical pain, the psychological agony and the financial devastation of dying. Terminally ill persons who have had control over their living expect to have control over their dying.

8.02) Procedures

After receiving a request for information, a **Dying Well Network** volunteer meets with the person making the request to gather preliminary information, to clarify what services are requested, and to specify what services **Dying Well Network** can and cannot provide. The volunteer gathers information from the terminally ill person, from family members, and from significant others present with the terminally or incurably ill person. Attention is given both to the right of the terminally ill person to make his or her own decisions regarding end of life and to the rights of those with whom the terminally ill person is related. The volunteer speaks only with those persons the terminally ill person designates. The terminally ill person must sign a Release of Information permitting the volunteer to share this information with the **Dying Well Network.**

After this preliminary information is collected the volunteer presents it to the **Dying Well Network** Board of Directors. The Board determines that the requesting person meets criteria for **Dying Well Network** to offer information. The Board may ask the volunteer to gather more information as needed.

If the terminally ill person meets criteria, **Dying Well Network** will provide information, and, possibly, presence at death. If the terminally ill person does not meet criteria, the person will be given referral(s) to other appropriate sources of care. The Board of Directors may have a medical consultant review the client's medical record to insure that the client is, within a reasonable medical certainty, terminally ill or suffering from a condition that is incurable and associated with severe, unrelenting suffering or agony. The Board of Directors, or a **Care Management Team** assigned, will review the case as often as necessary but at least once a month. The Board of Directors will provide the primary physician with information as necessary. The Board of Directors will continue to follow the client until the client dies or requests discontinuation of services from **Dying Well Network**.

Dying Well Network provides information to help a terminally ill person control his or her dying. **Dying Well Network** supplies information about how to control the time and manner of death. Information includes methods of dying. If requested, **Dying Well Network** will inform the terminally ill person about professional counselors and ordained religious leaders who will aid a terminally ill person to use verbal and spiritual methods of "letting go of life" in order to die well. **Dying Well Network** will inform terminally ill persons about volunteers who are willing to be with the terminally ill person at the time of death.

Because of the current legal situation, **Dying Well Network** cannot refer terminally ill persons to physicians or anyone else who may be willing to provide physical means to hasten dying.

Dying Well Network cannot and does not provide terminally ill persons the physical means to hasten death.

Dying Well Network maintains strict confidentiality.

8.03) Qualifications

A person who requests assistance in dying must meet the following criteria before **Dying Well Network** can offer information and presence:

1. The person must be an adult and mentally competent. **Dying Well Network** does not give information to minors or to persons who are incompetent.

2. The person must sign a Release of Information allowing the **Dying Well Network** volunteer to share information with the **Dying Well Network** and their consultant(s).

3. The person must sign Releases of Information so **Dying Well Network** personnel can receive information from the treating physician(s) and other past and present care-givers as appropriate, especially including Hospice.

4. The person must be diagnosed as terminally ill by a licensed physician or the person must have a condition that is incurable and associated with severe, unrelenting psychological agony or physical suffering even if not imminently terminal, for example, chronic, progressive multiple sclerosis.

5. The person must make his or her own decision and must not be coerced. Consultation with a certified or licensed professional mental health provider will be required if there is any doubt that the person's request is voluntary, rational and enduring. The consulting mental health provider will review the supporting

materials and may interview the person making the request for information.

6. The person must understand the condition, prognosis and the types of available treatments and comfort care as a part of informed consent. All reasonable treatment and comfort-oriented measures must have been tried or at least been considered.

7. When there is significant uncertainty about the person's medical condition or prognosis, a second opinion shall be sought and the uncertainty clarified as much as possible before a final decision is made about the person's request.

8. The person must sign an Informed Request form that acknowledges that he or she is aware of the current legal status of performing a suicide and of the jeopardy of those who are involved in the process in any way. This form will inform the terminally ill person that in the State of Washington a "civil commitment" law (RCW 71.05) states that a person who is imminently dangerous to himself or herself, as evidenced by intent or attempts to harm self as a result of a mental or emotional disorder, may receive involuntary psychiatric care. In the absence of such a disorder, Washington law does not address, reference or adjudicate an individual's attempt to die. More simply stated, if a person believes that a second person is attempting to kill himself or herself because of a mental illness, then the first person can request a Mental Health Professional to evaluate the second person for need of psychiatric treatment even if the second person does not want the evaluation or treatment.

9. The person will sign a form acknowledging that his or her physician(s) and/or treatment facility may choose to discontinue care when the person considers hastening death. If the physician(s) and/or facility discontinue(s) care then it is the person's responsibility to reinstate the relationship or find

alternate care. **Dying Well Network** can help the person find alternative sources of care which do not abandon or refer out a person who is planning to hasten death.

10. The person must be capable of understanding the nature of the information provided and its implications. The presence of depression is relevant if it affects the person's ability to make rational decisions. Depression is different than grief. In both grief and depression a person is reacting to losses, but in grief, unlike in depression, a person still maintains self-esteem. A person who is seeking information to control death is not necessarily depressed.

11. The person will sign a form acknowledging that the science of gentle, nonviolent suicide by overdose is not failure proof. Experience gained by the **Dying Well Network** and Compassion in Dying, another organization dedicated to helping terminally ill persons die well, dictates protocols which must be followed to insure the highest probability of dying well in a timely manner. Contrary to popular belief, death by overdose, even huge overdoses, frequently fails. **Dying Well Network** warns that do-it-yourself overdosing frequently fails, leaving the dying person even worse off and in a more desperate situation. The recipes listed in the "Drug Dosage Table" in Derek Humphry's book, <u>Final Exit</u>, are not failure proof. There are known failures even though the protocols were suggested and supplied in good faith by physicians who were "certain" that the overdose they prescribed would result in a peaceful, timely death. **Dying Well Network** adamantly advises against a terminally or incurably ill person attempting suicide by following recipes available from hearsay, books, pamphlets or on the Internet. **Dying Well Network** will not provide presence at death unless a mutually satisfactory protocol is planned and followed.

12. Informing family members is strongly recommended. Ideally, close family members should be an integral part of the decision-

making process and should understand and support the person's decision. The dying person must be careful about disclosure both for the sake of self and others. Disclosure to a person vehemently opposed to hastening death may make it difficult or impossible to complete. Disclosure to a person who would not be able to live with it afterwards is also contraindicated. If there is a dispute between the family and the dying person about whether or how to proceed, it may require the involvement of a counselor to mediate the differences. If requested, **Dying Well Network** may help find resolution or mediation. **Dying Well Network** reserves the right to refuse to be present at death if a family member or significant loved one is opposed to hastening death. If **Dying Well Network** is asked to be present at the time of death, we request that only the spouse or a significant loved one be present unless other arrangements have been made and agreed to in advance.

13. Cremation will follow death unless waived by **Dying Well Network**. In case of a criminal investigation **Dying Well Network** does not want to risk having the body exhumed. It could be problematic for **Dying Well Network** and certainly would be difficult for the surviving loved ones. Once physician aid-in-dying is legal, this qualification will be dropped.

8.04) Services

Dying Well Network offers information about hastening death but does not give assistance. If requested, **Dying Well Network** will be present at the deathing. **Dying Well Network** encourages persons who want to hasten death to request assistance, first, from their own physician. If that physician is unwilling, **Dying Well Network** will help find physician(s) who will provide aid-in-dying.

Dying Well Network provides services only within the immediate area of Spokane, Washington and Coeur d'Alene, Idaho.

8.05) Cost

Dying Well Network is a non-profit organization that does not charge a fee for information, but accepts contributions. All the board members, officers and consultants of **Dying Well Network** volunteer their time without compensation. **Dying Well Network** is grateful for charitable donations.

8.06) How to contact Dying Well Network

Dying Well Network
PO Box 880
Spokane, WA 99210-0880

Phone (509) 926-2457

Fax (509) 927-8819

If you have internet access you may visit **Dying Well Network's** webpage at <http://www.ior.com/~jeffw/homepage.htm>. (Don't type the < > symbols, just what's between them.)

ABOUT THE AUTHOR

Rob Neils, Ph.D., is a professional clinical psychologist licensed in Washington state and is in private practice in Spokane, Washington.

He has accomplished the following tasks relating to helping people live and die well:

1. Conducted the world's first group psychotherapy for terminally ill persons. (Parenthetically, the first person to die in that group was his co-therapist who had not known he was terminally ill!)

2. Wrote the world's first doctoral dissertation on the treatment of grief.

3. Wrote the first psychological treatment plan targeting "dying well, and hopefully earlier" as the desired outcome of therapy.

4. Attended the Lutheran School of Theology for 3½ years studying systematic theology and pastoral care, focusing on death and dying.

5. Wrote Death With Dignity FAQs (Frequently Asked Questions) and other **Dying Well Network** material.

6. Is constructing "Dr. Scisors: Death Readiness: Short Clinical Indicator Scale Of Rational Suicide," a psychological test to help clinicians differentially diagnose persons considering rational versus irrational suicide.

7. Wrote "How People Grieve," a bulletin of the Cooperative Extension Service of Montana State University.

8. Conducted workshops throughout Montana and other western states for more than 70,000 persons on "How People Grieve."

9. Was a psychology intern on the Oncology (Cancer) Unit at Fresno Community Hospital for one year using psychotherapy to aid persons while in treatment for cancer or dying.

10. Was Treasurer and on the Board of Directors for Washington Citizens for Death With Dignity, an organization which brought the first ever initiative on physician aid-in-dying to the vote of the people.

11. Has been a consultant to Hospice of Spokane and is a consultant to hospices throughout southern British Columbia, Canada.

12. Organized and is president of **Dying Well Network**, a non-profit organization based in Spokane, Washington.

13. Gave a Declaration in Gary Lee, et al. v. Douglas, et al., the injunction against Oregon's Measure 16.

14. Was an original plaintiff in the Compassion In Dying et al. v. Washington State until the time the suit was filed. He was dropped because legal considerations required the lawsuit to be tightly focused on <u>physician</u> aid-in-dying using pharmaceuticals rather than on psychological or religious verbal means to hasten death.

15. Encouraged the American and Washington State Psychological Associations to join as Amicus to the Compassion In Dying et. al. v. Washington State.

16. Wrote the first draft of the "End of Life Decisions" statement for the Social Issues and Human Rights committee of the Washington State Psychological Association.

17. Was chief psychologist at Eastern State Hospital. He has done hundreds of involuntary treatment evaluations and has testified throughout Eastern Washington concerning sanity and competency.

18. Is on the Board of Directors of the Spokane Memorial Society.

19. Through **Dying Well Network** requested the Unitarian-Universalist Church of Spokane to consider offering sanctuary for a terminally or incurably ill person intending to hasten death.

20. Is an expert witness weekly for Social Security Disability Hearings before Administrative Law Judges.

21. Presently is in private practice at North Pines Counseling, doing general psychological practice while specializing in grief, death, dying and catastrophic events.

Has been, and continues to be, present with terminally and incurably ill persons as they hastened death.

Dr. Neils gives presentations and conducts workshops on grief and the Death With Dignity movement. He uses actual case histories to describe dying poorly and dying well. He is respectful of differences of opinion and religious orientations. He rationally and warmly advocates a pro-choice stance on the right to die. He uses humor, poetry and narrative to move his audiences to greater awareness and insight into dealing with death, whether a loved one's or one's own.

REFERENCES

BOOKS

American Psychiatric Association, *Diagnostic and Statistical Manual of Mental Disorders, Fourth Edition.* Washington, DC, American Psychiatric Association, 1994.

Battin, Margaret Pabst, *Ethical Issues in Suicide.* Prentice Hall, Englewood Cliffs, New Jersey, 1995.

Becker, Ernest, *The Denial of Death.* Free Press, New York, 1973.

Bronowski, Jacob, *The Ascent of Man.* Little, Brown and Company, Boston, 1973.

Docker, Chris & Smith, Cheryl, *Departing Drugs: An International Guidebook to Self-Deliverance for the Terminally Ill.* Right to Die Society of Canada, P.O. Box 2422, Eugene, Oregon 97402, 1993.

Feinstein, David, *Rituals for Living and Dying: From Life's Wounds to Spiritual Awakening.* Harper, San Francisco, 1990.

Foos-Graber, Anya, *Deathing: An Intelligent Alternative for the Final Moments of Death.* Nicolas-Hays, Inc. York Beach, Maine, 1992.

Frankl, Viktor, *Man's Search for Meaning.* Simon & Schuster, New York, 1970.

Gilligan, Carol, *In a Different Voice: Psychological Theory and Women's Development.* Harvard University Press, Cambridge, Massachusetts, 1993.

Gibran, Kahil, *The Prophet.* Knopf, New York, 1967.

Humphry, Derek, *Dying With Dignity: What You Need to Know About Euthanasia.* St. Martin's Paperbacks, New York, 1993.

Humphry, Derek, *Final Exit: The Practicalities of Self-Deliverance and Assisted Suicide for the Dying.* Carol Publishing, Secaucus, New Jersey, 1991.

Jamison, Stephen, *Final Acts of Love: Families, Friends and Assisted Dying.* Putnam, New York, 1995.

Keleman, Stanley, *Living Your Dying.* Randomhouse, New York, 1974.

Levine, Stephen, *Healing Into Life and Death.* Anchor Books, New York, 1987.

Levine, Stephen, *Who Dies? An Investigation of Conscious Living and Conscious Dying.* Anchor Press/Doubleday, Garden City, New York, 1982.

LeShan, Eda, *Learning to Say Goodbye: When a Parent Dies.* Macmillan, New York, 1976.

McWilliams, Peter et al., *How to Survive the Loss of a Love.* Bantam Books, New York, 1979.

Misbin, Robert I., *Euthanasia: The Good of the Patient, the Good of Society.* University Publishing Group, Frederick, Maryland, 1972.

Ogden, Russel D., *Euthanasia, Assisted Suicide & AIDS.* Perreault/Goedman Publishing, Pitt Meadows, British Columbia, Canada, 1994.

Quill, Timothy E., *Death and Dignity: Making Choices and Taking Charge.* Norton, New York, 1993.

Rinpoche, Sogyal, *The Tibetan Book of Living and Dying.* Harper, San Francisco, 1994.

Risley, Robert L., *Death With Dignity: A New Law Permitting Physician Aid-In-Dying.* Hemlock Society, Eugene, Oregon, 1989.

Shavelson, Lonny, *A Chosen Death: The Dying Confront Assisted Suicide.* Simon & Schuster, New York, 1995.

Singer, Peter, *Rethinking Life and Death: The Collapse of Our Traditional Ethics.* St. Martin's Press, New York, 1995.

Spiegel, Yorick, *The Grief Process: Analysis and Counseling.* Abingdon, Nashville, Tennessee, 1977.

Werth, James L., Jr., *Rational Suicide? Implications for Mental Health Professionals.* Taylor & Francis, Washington, D.C., 1996.

Wilcox, Sandra and Sutton, Marilyn, *Understanding Death and Dying: An Interdisciplinary Approach.* Alfred Publishing, Port Washington, New York, 1977.

ARTICLES

Asch, D. A., *The Role of Critical Care Nurses in Euthanasia and Assisted Suicide.* New England Journal of Medicine 1996; 334:1374-1379.

Bachman, Jerald G. et al., *Attitudes of Michigan Physicians and the Public toward Legalizing Physician-Assisted Suicide and Voluntary Euthanasia.* New England Journal of Medicine 1996; 334:303-309.

Back, A. L. et al., *Physician-Assisted Suicide and Euthanasia in Washington State: Patient Requests and Physician Response.* Journal of the American Medical Association 1996; 275:919-925.

Baron, Charles H. et al., *A Model State Act to Authorize and Regulate Physician-Assisted Suicide.* Harvard Journal on Legislation. 1996;33(1):1-34.

Cohen, J. S. et al., *Attitudes toward Assisted Suicide and Euthanasia among Physicians in Washington State.* New England Journal of Medicine 1994; 331:89-94.

Coyle, N. et al., *Character of terminal illness in the advanced cancer patient: Pain and other symptoms during the last four weeks of life.* Journal of Pain Symptom Management 1990; 5(2):78-82.

Emanuel, E. J. & Emanuel, L. L., *The Economics of Dying: The Illusion of Cost Savings at the End of Life.* New England Journal of Medicine 1994; 330:540-544.

Griffiths, John, *The Regulation of Euthanasia and Related Medical Procedures that Shorten Life in the Netherlands*. Medical Law International 1994; 1:137-158.

Quill, Timothy, *Death and Dignity: A Case of Individualized Decision Making*. New England Journal of Medicine 1991; 324:691-694.

Knaus, William A., et al., *A Controlled Trial to Improve Care for Seriously Ill Hospitalized Patients*. Journal of the American Medical Association 1995: 274:1591-1598.

Knaus, William A., et al., *Short Term Mortality Predictions for Critically Ill Hospitalized Adults: Science and Ethics*. Science 1991; 254:389-394.

Lee, Melinda, et al., *Legalizing Assisted Suicide – Views of Physicians in Oregon*. New England Journal of Medicine 1996; 334:310-315.

Liaschenko, J. & Davis, A. J., *Nurses and Physicians on Nutritional Support: A Comparison*. Journal of Medical Philosophy 1991; 16:259-283.

Lukes, Paul, *Letter to the Editor*, in, Helen Voorhis (ed), *Timelines*. Hemlock Society, Denver, Colorado, March-April, 1996, pp. 8-9.

National Association of Social Workers, Delegate Assembly, *Client Self-determination in End-of-Life Decisions*. In *Social Work Speaks (3rd ed.)*, NASW Press, Washington, DC 20002-4241, 1994 (pp. 58-61).

Neils, Rob, *How People Grieve*. Cooperative Extension Service, Montana State University, 1971.

Shapiro, R. S. et al., *Willingness to Perform Euthanasia: A Survey of Physician Attitudes*. Archives of Internal Medicine 1994; 154:575-584.

Van der Wal, Gerrit & Dillman R. *Euthanasia in the Netherlands*. British Medical Journal 1994;308:1346-1349.

Wanzer, Sidney H. et al., *The Physician's Responsibility toward Hopelessly Ill Patients: A Second Look.* New England Journal of Medicine 1989; 320:844-849.

Washington State Psychological Association, Social Issues and Human Rights committee, *Policy Statement: End-of-Life Decisions.* P.O. Box 2016, Edmonds, Washington 98206, 1996.

COURT DATA

Brief for the Washington Psychological Association, The American Counseling Association, the Associations for Gay, Lesbian and Bisexual Issues in Counseling and a Coalition of Mental Health Professionals as Amici Curiae Supporting Respondent in the Supreme Court of the United States, October Term, 1996. Compassion in Dying v. State of Washington, District Court, C94-119R, May 3, 1994. (Judge Rothstein)

Compassion in Dying v. State of Washington, Ninth Circuit Court of Appeals, 96 C.D.O.S. 1507, March 6, 1996. (Judge Reinhardt)

Quill v. Vacco, Second Circuit Court of Appeals, 90-7028, April 2, 1996. (Judge Miner)